The 101 Greatest Weapons of All Times

101 GREAT FIGHTERS

Edited by
Robert Jackson

ROSEN
PUBLISHING®

New York

This edition first published in 2010 by:

The Rosen Publishing Group, Inc.
29 East 21st Street
New York, NY 10010

Additional end matter copyright © 2010 by The Rosen Publishing Group, Inc.

Project Editor: Sarah Uttridge
Picture Research: Terry Forshaw and Kate Green
Design: Graham Curd

Library of Congress Cataloging-in-Publication Data

Jackson, Robert, 1941–
101 great fighters / Robert Jackson, editor.
    p. cm.—(The 101 greatest weapons of all times)
Includes index.
ISBN 978-1-4358-3597-9 (library binding)
1. Fighter planes—History—Juvenile literature. 2. Fighter planes—Juvenile literature. I. Title.
II. Title: One hundred one great fighters. III. Title: One hundred and one great fighters.
UG1242.F5J326 2010
623.74'64—dc22

2009032122

Manufactured in USA

Copyright © 2008 by Amber Books Ltd. First published in 2008 by Amber Books Ltd.

Picture Credits:
All photographs courtesy of **Art-Tech/Aerospace** except for the following:
Art-Tech/MARS: 15, 39, 57, 58, 74, 81, 87; **Dassault:** 103, 106; **Eurofighter:** 10, 109
NASA Dryden Flight Research Center: 66; **Saab:** 107; **U.S. Department of Defense:** 8, 79, 86, 89, 91, 92, 97, 99, 100, 104, 108, 110
All artworks courtesy of **Art-Tech/Aerospace**

Contents

Introduction

In World War I the fighter aircraft (or "scout," as the type was then known) essentially fought its battles over the front lines in western and eastern Europe. The two decades that separated World War I and World War II saw huge technological strides in the development of fighter aircraft – yet 15 of those years passed before designers finally accepted that the cantilever monoplane, with its single strong spar running from wingtip to wingtip and traversing the fuselage, was a far better proposition than the strut-and-wire-braced biplane. Consequently, it was the mid-1930s before the monoplane fighters that would play such an enormous part in the coming conflict began to leave the drawing boards of the world's major aircraft manufacturers.

Enclosed cockpits and retractable undercarriages improved comfort and speed respectively, and these new aircraft, such as the Messerschmitt 109, the Hawker Hurricane and the Supermarine Spitfire, proved their effectiveness in the early campaigns of World War II. In the Pacific theater, the Mitsubishi Zero reigned supreme until it met its match in the shape of the Grumman F6F Hellcat, while in Russia, new combat types like the Lavochkin La-5 could at last counter Germany's formidable Focke-Wulf Fw 190, which was at least the equal of Allied fighter types in the west, and better than most.

It was in the west that the decisive air battles were fought. Now, at last, the Allies had a fighter – the North American P-51 Mustang that could escort the bombers of the USAF all the way to Berlin and back, and face the sternest challenge of the last months of the war – the Messerschmitt Me 262 jet fighter being deployed in increasing numbers

The McDonnell F-4 Phantom was the "workhorse" of the USAF and US Navy during the most dangerous years of the Cold War.

from the autumn of 1944. The Me 262 was the shape of future conflict in the air, and its aerodynamic design would be reflected in the jet-powered combat aircraft of east and west that would appear in the early post-war years. There were other radical innovations, too: amazing aircraft such as the rocket-powered Me 163, which while it was as much a danger to its pilots as to the enemy, did still lay the foundation for high-speed rocket research after the war.

In the wake of World War II came the Korean War, which saw the world's first jet-versus-jet combats with American F-86 Sabres battling Russian MiG-15s. A decade later, the eyes of the world were focused on the war in Vietnam, in which the United States Air Force, Navy and Marine Corps suffered losses in attacks on the heavily-defended north, where F-4 Phantoms battled with MiG-21s and American pilots found themselves locked in combat with highly competent and skilled adversaries.

These limited wars produced lessons in fighter evolution, culminating in aircraft such as the formidable F-22, which today represents the pinnacle of combat aircraft technology.

This book presents 101 of the world's finest fighters in chronological order, from the biplanes that battled over Flanders during World War I to the potency of today's advanced jets.

Left: Although always overshadowed by the Spitfire, the Hawker Hurricane fought its way through World War II from Norway to Burma.

Below: The huge amount of ordnance that can be carried by a modern combat aircraft is evident in this photograph of a Eurofighter Typhoon.

Fokker E.III

The Fokker monoplane was the first dedicated fighter aircraft to see operational service, and for months it made Allied reconnaissance flights into German territory virtual suicide missions.

COUNTRY OF ORIGIN: Germany

TYPE: single-seat fighting scout

POWERPLANT: one 100 hp (75 kW) Oberusel U.I 9-cylinder rotary engine

PERFORMANCE: maximum speed 83 mph (134 km/h); service ceiling 3500 m (11,500 ft); endurance 2 hrs 45 mins

WEIGHTS: empty 1100 lb (500 kg); loaded 1400 lb (635 kg)

DIMENSIONS: span 31 ft 3 in (9.52 m); length 23 ft 11 in (7.3 m); height 9 ft 6 in (3.12 m); wing area 172 sq ft (16 sq m)

ARMAMENT: one fixed forward-firing .312 in (7.92 mm) LMG 08/15 machine gun

The Fokker monoplane was a very simple and functional design, as this photograph of a flying replica shows.

Anthony Fokker designed and built his first aircraft in 1912. The Fokker Spin was a tandem-seat monoplane with considerable dihedral, and had no lateral control. It was rejected by the British, who considered it "badly built," although this probably stemmed from the general dislike of monoplanes among British officialdom, not scientific examination. So Fokker offered his services to Germany, which built his M.5 monoplane in large numbers.

The stuff of legend

In April 1915 Roland Garros' aircraft, with his self-designed bullet deflector gear, fell into German hands, prompting them to develop a more effective interrupter gear. This was fitted to a short-span M.5k scout to produce the E.I, and from April until the end of December 1915 the

Fokker monoplane was the scourge of Allied pilots on the Western Front. The "Fokker Scourge" began on July 1, 1915, when Lieutenant Kurt Wintgens of Feldflieger Abteilung 6b, flying the Fokker M.5k, shot down a French Morane monoplane. There was no doubt about this, but since the Morane fell inside French lines it was not upheld by the German High Command. Meanwhile, the production Fokker E.I had begun to reach the front-line German units in June. The small number of machines available, flown by pilots whose names would soon become legend, among them Lieutenants Oswald Böelcke and Max Immelmann, both of Feldflieger Abteilung 62, made their presence felt.

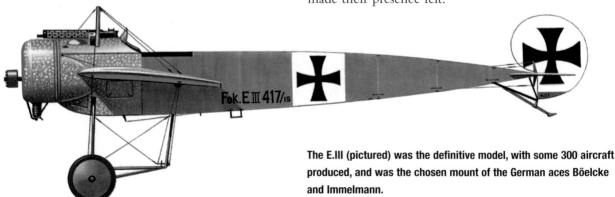

The E.III (pictured) was the definitive model, with some 300 aircraft produced, and was the chosen mount of the German aces Böelcke and Immelmann.

Sopwith Camel

Although it had a number of vicious tendencies, the Sopwith Camel (first issued to No. 4 Squadron RNAS and No. 70 Squadron RFC on the Western Front in July 1917) was a superb fighting machine in the hands of a skilled pilot.

COUNTRY OF ORIGIN: United Kingdom

TYPE: single-seat fighting scout

POWERPLANT: one 130 hp (97 kW) Clerget rotary piston engine

PERFORMANCE: maximum speed 115 mph (185 km/h); service ceiling 19,000 ft (5790 m); endurance 2 hrs 30 mins

WEIGHTS: empty 929 lb (421 kg); maximum take-off 1453 lb (659 kg)

DIMENSIONS: span 28 ft (8.53 m); length 18 ft 9 in (5.72 m); height 8 ft 6 in (2.59 m); wing area 231 sq ft (21.46 sq m)

ARMAMENT: two fixed forward-firing .303 in (7.7 mm) Vickers machine guns; plus up to four 25 lb (11.3 kg) bombs carried on fuselage sides

This Camel has a machine gun mounted over the upper wing for use against Zeppelins in its night-fighter role.

The Sopwith Triplane had only been in service for six months when its replacement, the Camel, began to arrive in service. Perhaps the most famous aircraft of World War I, the Camel was so-called because of its distinctive "humped" back, and between June 1917 and November 1918 it destroyed at least 3000 enemy aircraft, a greater total than that attained by any other aircraft.

Trainee-pilot killer

The Camel was a clear linear descendant of the Pup and Triplane, but its combat performance was achieved at some cost to the peerless handling of the earlier types. In inexperienced hands the Camel could bite, and the engine's torque was such that it had a nasty tendency to flip suddenly to the left on take-off. Trainee-pilot casualties were high, but once mastered it was a superb dogfighter. Total production was about 5490 aircraft, many of which served with foreign air arms. The Camel F.1 also equipped a number of Home Defense squadrons, the night-fighter version being equipped with a pair of Lewis guns mounted on the upper wing center section. The final production version was the Camel 2F.1, designed for shipboard operation. As well as being flown from the aircraft carriers HMS *Furious* and HMS *Pegasus*, the 2F.1 could also be catapulted from platforms erected on the gun turrets and forecastles of other capital ships, or launched from a lighter towed behind a destroyer.

The Sopwith Camel has justifiably been described as the "Spitfire" of World War I, although it did not share the later fighter's excellent handling qualities.

Pfalz D.III

The Pfalz D.III, issued to the Jagdstaffeln on the Western Front from August 1917, was somewhat inferior in performance to its contemporary Albatros and Fokker scouts, but it was built stronger and was more streamlined.

The gap between the Pfalz's upper wing and the fuselage was kept to a minimum, giving the pilot a good all-around field of view.

The Pfalz Flugzeug-Werke GmbH began building aircraft in 1913. At first it built Morane monoplanes and other types under license. The D.III was a totally fresh design into which company designer Robert Thelen poured much experience gained in 1916–17 with the production of LFG-Roland fighters.

Robust plane with a poor climb rate

Though fractionally inferior in performance to the best contemporary Albatros and Fokker scouts, the III and IIIa were strong aircraft. The monocoque fuselage was well streamlined and owed much to Deperdussin construction principles. About 600 were built, the more powerful IIIa having rounded wings and tailplane, and the guns located on top of the nose to allow for easier maintenance. A single example of an experimental triplane version of the D.III was built, but this was never flown. The D.III/IIIa was initially issued to home defense units in Bavaria in August 1917. By the end of the year 276 D.IIIs and 114 D.IIIas were in service, and from then on the former was gradually replaced by the latter, of which 433 were with front-line units in April 1918. Forty-six Jagdstaffeln (Jastas) received some D.III/IIIas, but only about a dozen were fully equipped with the type. The Pfalz does not seem to have been popular with many pilots, although some of Germany's leading air aces flew it. This was possibly because its rate of climb was poor compared with that of other German types like the Fokker D.VII, with which it was progressively replaced in the summer of 1918.

COUNTRY OF ORIGIN: Germany

TYPE: single-seat fighter

POWERPLANT: one 180hp (134kW) Mercedes D.IIIa inline piston engine

PERFORMANCE: maximum speed 103 mph (165 km/h); service ceiling 17,000 ft (5180 m); range 217 miles (350 km)

WEIGHTS: empty 1,653 lb (750 kg); maximum take-off 2061 lb (935 kg)

DIMENSIONS: span 30 ft 10 in (9.4 m); length 22 ft 9.5 in (6.95m); height 8 ft 9 in (2.67 m); wing area 237.89 sq ft (22.1 sq m)

ARMAMENT: two fixed forward-firing (.312 in) 7.92 mm LMG 08/15 machine guns

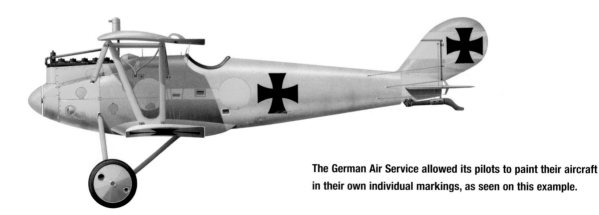

The German Air Service allowed its pilots to paint their aircraft in their own individual markings, as seen on this example.

Fokker D.VII

The Fokker D.VII was the first of a series of new German fighter types that, had they been available a few weeks earlier, might have wrested air superiority from the Allies during the German spring offensives of 1918.

COUNTRY OF ORIGIN: Germany	
TYPE: single-seat fighting scout	
POWERPLANT: one 185hp (138kW) B.M.W III 6-cylinder inline piston engine	
PERFORMANCE: maximum speed 124 mph (200 km/h); service ceiling 22,965 ft (7000 m); endurance 1 hr 30 mins	
WEIGHTS: empty 1620 lb (735 kg); maximum take-off 1940 lb (880 kg)	
DIMENSIONS: span 29 ft 2 in (8.9m); length 22 ft 9 in (6.95 m); height 9 ft (2.75 m); wing area 221 sq ft (20.5 sq m)	
ARMAMENT: two fixed forward-firing .312 in (7.92 mm) LMG 08/15 machine guns	

The D.VII was modified to improve its stability in a dive, but its main advantage was how well it performed at high altitude.

The early "D" series scouts (D.I to D.VI) were unremarkable aircraft produced by Fokker between August 1915 and late 1917, with undistinguished service careers and dull performance. They were eclipsed by the D.VII designed in late 1917 by a team led by Fokker's Chief Engineer Rheinhold Platz, in time for the German standard fighter competition of January 1918.

Training future Luftwaffe pilots

The D.VII proved vastly superior to any of the others. After modification with a longer fuselage and fixed fin it was put into production. The first unit to receive it was Manfred von Richtofen's unit JG I, which was commanded by

Hermann Göring after April 1918. About one thousand of this aircraft had been built by the time of the Armistice. At the end of the war, Anthony Fokker smuggled 400 engines and the components of 120 aircraft, most of them D.VIIs, out of Germany into Holland, where he set up a production line. Post-war, the D.VII saw service in the Dutch East Indies, Poland, the USA, Switzerland, Belgium, Sweden, Romania, Russia, Denmark, Finland and Italy. Some of these aircraft were re-engined with 250 hp (186 kW) BMW or 230 hp (172 kW) Siddeley motors. Russia was one of the most important customers, acquiring 92 D.VIIs, many of which were used to train German pilots who would form the nucleus of the future Luftwaffe in secret at the Lipetsk flying school.

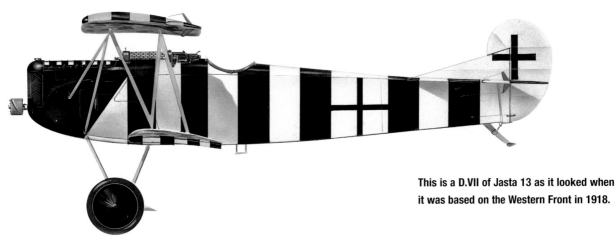

This is a D.VII of Jasta 13 as it looked when it was based on the Western Front in 1918.

Gloster Gamecock

The Gloster Gamecock prototype, the last wooden biplane fighter designed for the RAF, first flew in February 1925, and the type equipped five RAF squadrons starting in May of 1926.

COUNTRY OF ORIGIN: United Kingdom

TYPE: single-seat biplane fighter

POWERPLANT: one 425hp (317kW) Bristol Jupiter VI 9-cylinder radial engine

PERFORMANCE: maximum speed 155 mph (249 km/h); service ceiling 22,000 ft (6705 m); endurance 2 hrs

WEIGHTS: empty 1930 lb (875 kg); maximum take-off 2863 lb (1299 kg)

DIMENSIONS: span 29 ft 9 in (9.08 m); length 19 ft 8 in (5.99 m); height 9 ft 8 in (2.95 m); wing area 264 sq ft (24.53 sq m)

ARMAMENT: two fixed forward-firing .303 in (7.7 mm) Vickers Mk I machine guns

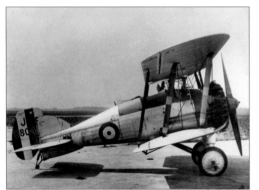

The Gamecock was very popular with its pilots, as it was very light and responsive on the controls.

The Gloster Gamecock was a development of the Mk III Grebe, built to Air Ministry Specification 27/23. It differed from the Grebe by way of its Bristol Jupiter engine, which replaced the unreliable Armstrong Siddeley Jaguar. Other changes included improved ailerons, refined fuselage contours and internally mounted machine guns.

Tough and reliable craft

It was first flown in February 1925, and 100 were acquired by the RAF, remaining in service until 1931. Its wood-and-fabric construction was unremarkable, but the Gamecock was a tough and reliable aircraft, able to survive almost anything thrown at it. The Gamecock Mk II (three built) had a revised center wing section. Gloster (as the company became known in 1926) supplied three Gamecock Mk IIs to Finland, which license-built another 15. The Gamecock's service life was relatively short-lived, partly because of an abnormally high accident rate; of the 90 Gamecocks built, 22 were lost in spinning or landing accidents. Yet this light, responsive plane was very popular with its pilots and it was a superb aerobatic aircraft. Its aerobatic displays in the hands of experienced squadron pilots did much to encourage a spirit of "air-mindedness" among the British public.

Finland was one export customer for the Gamecock. In Finnish service, the aircraft was known as the Kukko.

Bristol Bulldog

The Bristol Bulldog represented a considerable advance over earlier British biplane fighters, being significantly faster. It enjoyed a good deal of export success.

The Bulldog was produced in several configurations. This one has a spatted undercarriage and a ring-type engine cowling.

COUNTRY OF ORIGIN: United Kingdom

TYPE: single-seat biplane fighter

POWERPLANT: one 490 hp (365 kW) Bristol Jupiter VIIF radial piston engine

PERFORMANCE: maximum speed 174 mph (280 km/h); service ceiling 29,300 ft (8940 m); range 300 miles (482 km)

WEIGHTS: empty 2222 lb (1008 kg); maximum take-off 3490 lb (1583 kg)

DIMENSIONS: span 33 ft 10 in (10.3 m); length 25 ft 2 in (7.7 m); height 8 ft 9 in (2.7 m); wing area 307 sq ft (28.47 sq m)

ARMAMENT: two fixed forward-firing .303 in (7.7 mm) Vickers machine guns; underwing racks with provision for up to four 20 lb (9 kg) bombs

In September 1926 the British Air Ministry needed a new single-seat day/night fighter aircraft powered by a radial air-cooled engine and armed with two .303 Vickers machine guns. Nine submissions were received, most of them powered by Bristol's Jupiter radial engine.

Outdated but still scoring successes

The Bristol design was selected for development. The prototype Bulldog Mk I flew for the first time in May 1927, and after the fuselage had been lengthened entered production as the Bulldog Mk II. The first aircraft was delivered to No. 3 Squadron, RAF, in June 1929, powered by a 440 hp (328 kW) Bristol Jupiter engine. The Bulldog eventually equipped ten RAF home defense squadrons, the main version being the Mk IIA, which featured a wider undercarriage and other modifications. The Bulldog also served in small numbers with the air forces of Denmark, Estonia, Finland, Latvia, Siam and Sweden, 456 being built in total. Some Finnish Bulldogs fought in the Russo-Finnish "Winter War" of 1939-40, registering some success against Soviet aircraft, but by that time they were hopelessly outdated.

The Bulldog was another British type used by the Finnish Air Force, the majority being fitted with skis.

Boeing PW-9C

One of the first post-WWI US fighter aircraft to enter service was the Boeing PW-9 (the designation signifying Pursuit, Water-cooled engine), a small and maneuverable machine powered by a 435 hp (324 kW) Curtiss D-12 engine.

COUNTRY OF ORIGIN: USA

TYPE: single-seat biplane fighter

POWERPLANT: one 435 hp (324.3 kW) Curtiss D-12D 12-cylinder V-type engine

PERFORMANCE: maximum speed 158 mph (254 km/h)

WEIGHTS: empty 2400 lb (1082 kg); maximum take-off 3170 lb (1438 kg)

DIMENSIONS: span 32 ft (9.75 m); length 23 ft 1 in (7.04 m); height 8 ft 8 in (2.64 m)

ARMAMENT: one 0.5 in (12.7 mm) and one 0.3 in (7.62 mm) machine gun in upper front fuselage

The Boeing PW-9 was one of the first fighters to enter service with the US Army Air Corps.

Developed as a private venture under the designation Boeing Model 15, the prototype flew for the first time on April 29, 1923. The USAAC placed its first production orders, totalling 30 aircraft, in 1924. Deliveries, to USAAC units in Hawaii and the Philippines, began in October 1925. Twenty-five more fighters, with minor modifications, were ordered as PW-9As; these were followed by 15 PW-9Bs. In early 1928, the prototype of a new fighter, developed jointly by the USN and Boeing in the course of the preceding year, appeared. This was the F3B-1, 74 of which were delivered from 1929 for service on board the USS *Langley*, *Lexington* and *Saratoga*. It was followed by the F4B, which was also offered to the US Army Air Corps, who ordered nine examples

under the designation P-12, plus a tenth aircraft, the XP-12A. In all, the USAAC took delivery of 90 P-12Bs, 96 P-12Cs and 110 P-12Es, which entered service in 1931 with more powerful engines and a metal fuselage; and 25 P-12Fs, which again had uprated engines.

End of the biplane fighter era
The service life of the P-12/F-4B series of fighter covered the most potentially dangerous years of the inter-war period; but those years also marked the end of the biplane fighter's era. The first US all-metal monoplane fighter design was the Boeing P-26, which first flew in March 1932. Deliveries of production P-26As to the USAAC, affectionately nicknamed "Peashooter" by pilots, began at the end of 1933. The P-26 became standard pursuit equipment in Hawaii and the Panama Canal area.

Deliveries of the PW-9C to USAAC units in the Philippines and Hawaii began in October 1925.

PZL P.11 and P.24

The P.24 appeared in 1933 and was similar to the P.11 but had a 770 hp (574 kW) Gnome-Rhone 14K engine and an enclosed cockpit. It never served in the Polish Air Force, but was used by Turkey, Romania, Greece and Bulgaria.

COUNTRY OF ORIGIN: Poland

TYPE: (P.24F) single-seat fighter

POWERPLANT: one 970 hp (723 kW) Gnome-Rhône 14N-07 14-cylinder two-row radial engine

PERFORMANCE: maximum speed 267 mph (430 km/h); climb to 16,405 ft (5000 m) in 5 minutes 40 seconds; service ceiling 34,450 ft (10,500 m); range 435 miles (700 km)

WEIGHTS: empty 2937 lb (1332 kg); maximum take-off 4409 lb (2000 kg)

DIMENSIONS: span 35 ft .75 in (10.68 m); length 24 ft 11.5 in (7.6 m); height 8 ft 10.25 in (2.69 m)

ARMAMENT: two .787 in (20 mm) fixed forward-firing cannon and two .312 in (7.92 mm) fixed forward-firing machine guns on the leading edges of the wing, plus an external bomb load of 88 lb (40 kg)

The PZL P.24 was the last in a line of the company's high-wing monoplane fighters, all of which were outclassed by 1939.

Poland's best fighter at the time of the 1939 Germany invasion, the P.24 was a more powerfully engined development of the P.11, itself an upgraded Bristol Mercury-engined version of the P.7 with the Bristol Jupiter engine. All three types were therefore braced gull-wing monoplanes with fixed landing gear.

Military budget cuts

The PZL P.11 first flew in September 1931, with deliveries beginning in 1934. Most P.11s were powered by Bristol Mercury engines, built under license by Skoda; the definitive version of the fighter was the P.11c, of which

175 were built. The P.11 was to have been replaced by a low-wing fighter monoplane, the P.50 Jastrzeb (Hawk), in a major expansion scheme, but cuts in the military budget resulted in the cancellation of an order for 300 P.50s, and more P.11s were purchased instead. They suffered heavy losses during the German invasion. The P.11b was an export model for Romania, which also built a small number of the type under license. As first flown in 1933, the P.24 introduced the more powerful Gnome-Rhône 14K engine, spatted main landing-gear wheels, and a strengthened structure. About 300 aircraft were built. The main variants were the P.24A with cannon and an enclosed cockpit, the P.24B with modified wheel spats, the P.24C development of the P.24A with machine gun armament, the P.24E with an uprated engine, and the P.24F and P.24G improved versions of the P.24A.

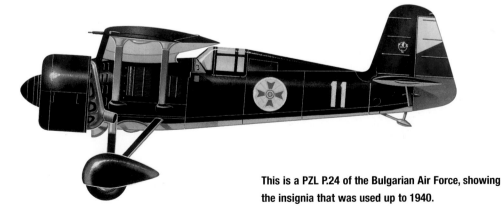

This is a PZL P.24 of the Bulgarian Air Force, showing the insignia that was used up to 1940.

Polikarpov I-15 and I-153

The I-15 was a first-rate combat aircraft and was subsequently to prove its worth in air fighting, being able to out-turn almost every aircraft that opposed it in action. It was the last single-seat fighter biplane to be series-produced in the Soviet Union.

The Polikarpov I-15 was a rugged and versatile fighter, but its biplane configuration soon rendered it obsolete.

From 1933, Nikolai Nikolayevich Polikarpov planned the I-15 as successor to his I-5 biplane fighter with a gulled upper wing (to improve the pilot's forward fields of vision) and a powerplant of one Wright R-1820-F Cyclone radial piston engine. The I-15 entered service in 1934. These were complemented and supplanted by the 2408 I-15bis (otherwise I-152), aircraft that were built, many of which were still in use at the time of Germany's 1941 invasion of the USSR. The I-15bis had the improved M-25V engine

This is one of many I-15s supplied to the Spanish Republican Air Force in the 1930s. The type fought in the Spanish Civil War.

in a longer-chord cowling, a conventional upper wing, greater fuel capacity, and doubled gun firepower.

Modernizing the I-15bis

Otherwise known as the I-15ter, the I-153 was first flown in 1938 as an attempt to modernize the I-15bis by reducing drag. The two most important changes were a reversion to the type of gulled upper wing used on the I-15, and the use of manually operated retractable main landing gear units. It built to the extent of 3437 aircraft and entered service in time for participation in the border incident with Japan in 1939. It was also heavily involved in the Russo-Finnish "Winter War" of 1939–40, and in the early part of the German invasion of the USSR in 1941.

COUNTRY OF ORIGIN: USSR

TYPE: (I-15bis) single-seat fighter

POWERPLANT: one 750 hp (559 kW) M-25B nine-cylinder single-row radial engine

PERFORMANCE: maximum speed 230 mph (370 km/h); climb to 3280 ft (1000 m) in 1 minute 6 seconds; service ceiling 29,530 ft (9000 m); range about 329 miles (530 km)

WEIGHTS: empty 2888 lb (1310 kg); maximum take-off 3814 lb (1730 kg)

DIMENSIONS: span 33 ft 5.5 in (10.2 m); length 20 ft 9.25 in (6.33 m); height 7 ft 2.25 in (2.19 m)

ARMAMENT: four .3 in (7.62 mm) fixed forward-firing machine guns in the upper part of the forward fuselage, plus an external bomb load of 220 lb (100 kg)

Polikarpov I-16

The first Soviet fighter to incorporate armor plating around the pilot's cockpit, the I-16 attracted great interest among foreign observers when examples flew over Moscow's Red Square during the Air Parade of May 1, 1935.

COUNTRY OF ORIGIN: USSR

TYPE: (I-16 Tip 24) single-seat fighter and fighter-bomber

POWERPLANT: one 1100 hp (820 kW) Shvetsov M-63 nine-cylinder single-row radial engine

PERFORMANCE: maximum speed 304 mph (489 km/h); climb to 16,405 ft (5000 m) in 4 minutes; service ceiling 29,530 ft (9000 m); range 435 miles (700 km)

WEIGHTS: empty 3285 lb (1490 kg); maximum take-off 4619 lb (2095 kg)

DIMENSIONS: span 29 ft 6.33 in (9 m); length 20 ft 1.3 in (6.13 m); height 8 ft 5 in (2.57 m)

ARMAMENT: two .3 in (7.62 mm) fixed forward-firing machine guns in the upper part of the forward fuselage and two .3 in (7.62 mm) fixed forward-firing machine guns or two .787 in (20 mm) fixed forward-firing cannon in the leading edges of the wing, plus an external bomb and rocket load of 1102 lb (500 kg)

Landing the I-16 was not easy because of the bulky engine cowling, restricting the pilot's view.

Designed at much the same time as the I-15, the I-16 was a more advanced fighter in its basic concept. It was the USSR's first cantilever low-wing monoplane fighter with retractable main landing-gear units (although the landing gear had to be retracted by pumping a handle no fewer than 100 times). The type first flew in December 1933, revealing tricky handling characteristics, especially in the longitudinal plane as a result of its short fuselage.

10 main variants

The type entered large-scale production (7005 aircraft built) and saw service up to 1942, latterly suffering very heavy losses. The I-16 was produced in 10 main variants between the I-16 Tip 1 with the 480 hp (358 kW) M-22 radial engine and the definitive I-16 Tip 24 with a more powerful engine as well as much heavier, more diverse armament. In 1938 the I-16 Type 17 was tested, armed with two wing-mounted cannons. This version was produced in large numbers. Then, with the cooperation of the armament engineer B.G. Shpitalnii, Polikarpov built the TsKB-12P, the first aircraft in the world to be armed with two synchronized cannons firing through the propeller arc. Altogether, 6555 I-16s were built before production ended in 1940. I-16s fought in Spain, against the Japanese in the Far East, and against the Luftwaffe.

This I-16 bears the Cyrillic legend (For the USSR!) on its fuselage side. Such slogans were common in the Soviet Air Force.

Gloster Gladiator

Although outclassed by German and Italian monoplane fighters, the Gladiator, the last of the RAF's biplane fighters, was to render gallant service during the early months of the war in both Europe and the Middle East.

COUNTRY OF ORIGIN: United Kingdom

TYPE: (Gladiator Mk I) single-seat fighter

POWERPLANT: one 830 hp (619 kW) Bristol Mercury IX nine-cylinder single-row radial engine

PERFORMANCE: maximum speed 253 mph (407 km/h); climb to 15,000 ft (4570 m) in 5 minutes 40 seconds; service ceiling 32,800 ft (9995 m); range 428 miles (689km)

WEIGHTS: empty 3600 lb (1633 kg); maximum take-off 4592 lb (2083 kg)

DIMENSIONS: span 32 ft 3 in (9.83 m); length 27 ft 5 in (8.36 m); height 10 ft 7 in (3.22 m)

ARMAMENT: two .303 in (7.7 mm) fixed forward-firing machine guns in the sides of the forward fuselage, and two .303 in (7.7 mm) fixed forward-firing machine guns in the leading edges of the lower wing

The Gloster Gladiator fought valiantly in the early campaigns of WWII, but was no match for German and Italian monoplane fighters.

The last and finest biplane British fighter, the Gladiator was a conceptual development of the Gauntlet with improved features such as an enclosed cockpit, trailing-edge flaps and cantilever main landing-gear legs. The prototype flew in September 1934, and the first of 378 Gladiator Mk I fighters entered service in 1937 pending the large-scale advent of more advanced monoplane fighters.

Sole air defense of the island of Malta

The Gladiator Mk I was supplemented by the Gladiator Mk II, of which 311 were delivered with the Mercury VIIIA or VIIIAS engine. Some 38 of the aircraft were converted to Interim Sea Gladiator standard, paving the way for the carrierborne Sea Gladiator, of which 60 were completed. Three Sea Gladiators achieved fame for their defense of the island of Malta in 1940. The island had been under attack by the Italian Air Force since Italy entered the war in June 1940, and for nearly three weeks the Sea Gladiators provided the sole air defense. Originally intended for service on HMS *Glorious*, the carrier sailed for Norwegian waters without them and afterward they were shipped to Malta in crates, intended for HMS *Eagle*. Instead, they were used to form a fighter flight and fought alone until they were joined by a handful of Hurricanes on June 28. They were immortalized in the newspapers by the names "Faith, Hope and Charity." The Gladiator saw first-line service in northern Europe and the Mediterranean to 1940 and the middle of 1941.

This Gloster Gladiator wears the pre-war markings of No. 73 Squadron.

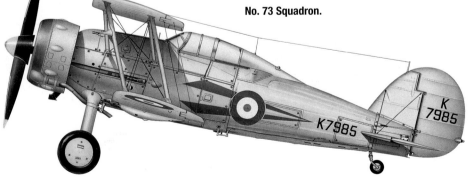

Curtiss P-36

Although not particularly a success story, the Curtiss P-36 had the distinction of being the USAAC's first "modern" monoplane fighter. Designed as a private venture, the prototype flew in May 1935.

COUNTRY OF ORIGIN: USA

TYPE: (P-36C) single-seat fighter

POWERPLANT: one 1200 hp (895 kW) Pratt & Whitney R-1830-17 14-cylinder two-row radial engine

PERFORMANCE: maximum speed 311 mph (500 km/h); climb to 15,000 ft (4570 m) in 4 minutes 54 seconds; service ceiling 33,700 ft (10,270 m); range 820 miles (1320 km)

WEIGHTS: empty 4620 lb (2096 kg); maximum take-off 6010 lb (2726 kg)

DIMENSIONS: span 37 ft 3.5 in (11.37 m); length 28 ft 10 in (8.79 m); height 9 ft 3 in (2.82 m)

ARMAMENT: one 0.5 in (12.7 mm) fixed forward-firing machine gun and one 0.3 in (7.62 mm) fixed forward-firing machine gun in the upper part of the forward fuselage, and two 0.3 in (7.62 mm) fixed forward-firing machine guns in the leading edges of the wing

The Curtiss P-36 was an excellent design, and gave a good account of itself in the Battle of France.

Anticipating the US Army's need for such an airplane, Curtiss designed and built the Model 75 (the USA's first "modern" monoplane fighter) as a private venture. It made its maiden flight in May 1935 with a Wright SGR-1670-G5 radial engine that was soon replaced by an uprated Wright R-1820-F Cyclone radial engine.

Serving abroad

The US Army then ordered three YP-36 aircraft for service trials, and this paved the way for 209 production aircraft in the form of 178 P-36A fighters that entered service from April 1938 and 31 P-36C fighters with two additional 0.3 in (7.12 mm) machine guns in the wing.

The type was also exported in Model 75A form to several countries including the UK, where the type was known as the Mohawk, and in downgraded Model 75 (or Hawk 75) form with fixed and spatted main landing-gear units. The Hawk 75As serving with the Armée de l'Air equipped five Groupes de Chasse and shot down over 300 enemy aircraft. Just before the collapse of France the five Curtiss Hawk Groupes were ordered to fly to North Africa, and 148 aircraft made the crossing. Between May 10 and June 24, 1940, Curtiss Hawk losses totalled 110 aircraft. A few Hawks were still flying as fighter trainers in 1946, although their operational career ended with the Allied landings in North Africa in November 1942.

The aircraft shown here wears the standard wartime olive-drab color scheme of the US Army Air Force and early 1942-type national insignia.

Messerschmitt Bf 109

Germany's standard single-seat fighter at the start of World War II, the Bf 109E was crucial to Luftwaffe success over the Polish, Scandinavian and northwest European battlefields between September 1939 and June 1940.

COUNTRY OF ORIGIN: Germany

TYPE: (Bf 109E-4) single-seat fighter

POWERPLANT: one 1175 hp (876 kW) Daimler-Benz DB 601Aa 12-cylinder inverted-Vee engine

PERFORMANCE: maximum speed 348 mph (560 km/h); climb to 19,685 ft (6000 m) in 7 minutes 45 seconds; service ceiling 34,450 ft (10,500 m); range 410 miles (660 km)

WEIGHTS: empty 4685 lb (2125 kg); normal take-off 5534 lb (2510 kg); maximum take-off 5875 lb (2665 kg)

DIMENSIONS: span 32 ft 4.5 in (9.87 m); length 28 ft 4.5 in (8.64 m); height 8 ft 2.33 in (2.5 m)

ARMAMENT: two .787 in (20 mm) fixed forward-firing cannons in the leading edges of the wing, and two .312 in (7.92 mm) fixed forward-firing machine guns in the upper part of the forward fuselage

This Messerschmitt Bf 109E-4 wears the mottled camouflage of the 1940-41 period.

When the type was committed at longer range against British fighters in the Battle of Britain its limitations became known. Entering service at the end of 1938 and with more than 4000 aircraft built, the Bf 109E "Emil" was in essence the Bf 109D revised with the more powerful DB 601 engine and cannon armament.

Improved but armament was too light
The main early variants were the Bf 109E-1 with the 1075 hp (801.5 kW) DB 601A-1 engine, Bf 109E-3 with an uprated engine, improved armor and provision for an engine-mounted .787 in (20 mm) cannon, and Bf 109E-4

with no engine cannon. Pilots regarded the Emil as one of the finest of the Me 109 models, and it was at least equal to early Spitfire models. Entering service in spring 1941, the Bf 109F marked the apogee of the Bf 109's development in terms of aerodynamic refinement (improved cowling, rounded wing tips and cantilever tailplane) and handling. These were achieved only at the expense of armament, which was thought too light, so production of the Bf 109F ended after the delivery of some 2200 aircraft. Still in production (23,500 aircraft) at the end of World War II, the Bf 109G was numerically the most important Bf 109 variant. Few of the pilots who flew it would dispute that improvements in the type's speed and firepower resulted in poorer overall handling qualities. The Bf 109G was delivered in pressurized (even-numbered) and unpressurized (odd-numbered) subvariants for service starting in the summer of 1942.

This is a Messerschmitt Bf 109E-4 of JG2 "Richthofen," Abbeville, 1941. Note the 'kill' markings on the tail fin.

Hawker Hurricane

The Spitfire has come to be remembered as the fighter that "won' the Battle of Britain, but it was the Hurricane that served in larger numbers and destroyed more German aircraft than the rest of the defenses combined.

COUNTRY OF ORIGIN: United Kingdom

TYPE: (Hurricane Mk I) single-seat fighter

POWERPLANT: one 1030 hp (768 kW) Rolls-Royce Merlin III 12-cylinder Vee engine

PERFORMANCE: maximum speed 324 mph (521 km/h); climb to 15,000 ft (5670 m) in 6 minutes 18 seconds; service ceiling 33,200 ft (10,120 m); range 445 miles (716 km)

WEIGHTS: empty 5085 lb (2308 kg); maximum take-off 6661 lb (3024 kg)

DIMENSIONS: span 40 ft (12.19 m); length 31 ft 4 in (9.55 m); height 13 ft 4.5 in (4.07 m)

ARMAMENT: eight .303 in (7.7 mm) fixed forward-firing machine guns in the leading edges of the wing

The Hurricane had the ability to absorb severe battle damage and still return to base.

The Hurricane was the first monoplane fighter to enter British service in the 1930s. Sidney Camm's design was not as advanced technically as the Spitfire and it had an unstressed covering largely of fabric. The prototype first flew in November 1935, and the Hurricane Mk I entered service late in 1937 with a two-blade fixed-pitch propeller that later gave way to a three-blade constant-speed unit.

Universal wing for ground–attack roles

Equipping 19 squadrons on the outbreak of World War II, the type flew with some 29 squadrons in August 1940, and production totalled about 3650 aircraft including 40, 489 and 150 examples of the Canadian-built Mks I, X and XI. Nearly 200 of the RAF Hurricanes were lost in the spring of 1940. In 1939 Hawker created an improved Hurricane Mk II with an uprated powerplant, heavier armament and enhancements such as metal-skinned wings and a three-blade propeller. These were also incorporated on later Mk I aircraft. Mk II production reached more than 7500 aircraft for service from September 1940 in variants such as the Mk IIA with eight 0.303 in (7.7 mm) machine guns, the Mk IIB with 12 0.303 in (7.7 mm) machine guns, the Mk IIC with four .767 in (20 mm) cannons and 1000 lb (454 kg) of external stores, and the anti-tank Mk IID produced in small numbers. Making its debut in 1943 with the designation Hurricane Mk IIE, used for the first 270 of the 794 aircraft. The Hurricane Mk IV was the final British production model and was the Hurricane Mk II with the Merlin 24 or 27 engine, 159 kg (350 lb) of additional armor, and with the so-called Universal Wing that allowed the optimization of the warplane for a number of ground–attack roles.

This is a Hawker Hurricane in the markings of South-East Asia Command. However, the red has been deleted from the insignia to prevent confusion with Japanese markings.

Mitsubishi A5M Claude

First flown in prototype form in January 1935, the Mitsubishi A5M was Japan's first carrierborne monoplane fighter and its appearance was very significant: it marked the end of Japanese dependence on foreign designs.

The A5M was a very maneuverable fighter, and proved itself in combat against various Western types like the Gloster Gladiator over China.

COUNTRY OF ORIGIN: Japan

TYPE: (A5M4) single-seat carrierborne and land-based fighter

POWERPLANT: one 785 hp (585 kW) Nakajima Kotobuki 41 or Kotobuki 41 Kai nine-cylinder single-row radial engine

PERFORMANCE: maximum speed 270 mph (435 km/h); climb to 9845 ft (3000 m) in 3 minutes 35 seconds; service ceiling 32,150 ft (9800 m); range 870 miles (1400 km)

WEIGHTS: empty 2874 lb (1263 kg); maximum take-off 4017 lb (1822 kg)

DIMENSIONS: span 36 ft 1.13 in (11 m); length 2 ft 8.36 in (7.57 m); height 10 ft 8.75 in (3.27 m)

ARMAMENT: two .303 in (7.7 mm) fixed forward-firing machine guns in the upper part of the forward fuselage, plus an external bomb load of 132 lb (60 kg)

It is impossible to overstate the importance of the A5M carrierborne fighter in the development of Japanese industry and military capabilities in the mid-1930s. With this type Japan moved from dependence on Western imports and thinking to a completely indigenous product that was Japan's first carrierborne monoplane fighter and also in every way comparable in terms of performance and capabilities with the best of its Western equivalents.

Popular with naval pilots

The A5M1 entered service in the spring of 1937. Production of the series, which departed first-line service in 1943, totalled 980 aircraft in the A5M1 to A5M4 series, the last with open cockpits. There were also 103 examples of the A5M4-K two-seat trainer development. In total it is estimated that nearly 1000 A5Ms were built, the aircraft proving very popular with naval pilots. The A5M was widely used in China, but with the exception of one attack on Davao in the Philippines the type did not see combat against the Allies. In China, the A5Ms mostly operated from the carrier *Hosho*, escorting bombers that were carrying out attacks on enemy bases in the Canton area. The fighting continued from July to December, when *Hosho* was placed in reserve and her air group dispersed for second-line duties.

This is a Mitsubishi A5M fighter of the *Akagi* carrier air group, 1938. The A5M was soon replaced by the A6M Zero.

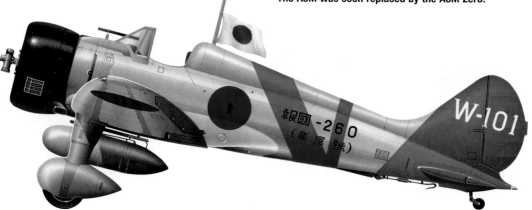

Morane-Saulnier MS.406

The Morane-Saulnier MS.405 was the first French fighter with a retractable undercarriage and enclosed cockpit. It flew for the first time at Villacoublay on August 8, 1935. Official trials of the MS.405 began in 1936.

COUNTRY OF ORIGIN: France

TYPE: (MS.406C.1) single-seat fighter

POWERPLANT: one 860 hp (641 kW) Hispano-Suiza 12Y-31 12-cylinder Vee engine

PERFORMANCE: maximum speed 304 mph (490 km/h); climb to 16,405 ft (5000 m) in 6 minutes 30 seconds; service ceiling 30,850 ft (9400 m); range 932 miles (1500 km)

WEIGHTS: empty 4127 lb (1872 kg); maximum take-off 6000 lb (2722 kg)

DIMENSIONS: span 34 ft 9.63 in (10.62 m); length 26 ft 9.33 in (8.17 m); height 10 ft 8 in (3.25 m) with the tail up

ARMAMENT: one .787 in (20 mm) fixed forward-firing cannon or .295 in (7.5 mm) fixed forward-firing machine gun in an engine installation, and two .295 (7.5 mm) fixed forward-firing machine guns in the leading edges of the wing

An early model MS.406 in flight. The aircraft had some curious features, such as a retractable radio aerial under the fuselage.

The MS.406 was France's first "modern" monoplane fighter with a cantilever low-set wing, enclosed cockpit and tailwheel landing gear that included inward-retracting main units. It was obsolete by World War II, however, and suffered heavy losses in combat against the superior fighters fielded by the Luftwaffe.

Fighter in the campaign against Britain in Syria

The type resulted from a 1934 requirement and was first conceived as the MS.405. The prototype flew in August 1935 and led to 15 MS.405C.1 pre-production fighters. There followed the MS.406C.1 production model of which an initial 1000 examples were ordered in March 1938. The MS.406 was built on two production lines, and construction of 1077 aircraft was completed between June 1938 and June 1940. Exports were made to Switzerland and Turkey, and captured aircraft were passed to Croatia and Finland. The only Vichy Air Force unit to be equipped with the MS.406 was GC I/7, based in the Levant, and in July 1941 it saw limited action against British forces during the campaign in Syria. The Morane fighter also equipped the 2e Escadrille of the Free French Air Force in North Africa before this unit converted to Hurricanes in 1941. Several MS.406s were still flying as late as 1947.

An MS.406 of Groupe de Chasse GC I/2 "Cigognes," Toul-Ochey, as it would have appeared in May 1940.

Messerschmitt Bf 110

The Messerschmitt Bf 110 was designed in response to a 1934 Reichsluftminsterium (RLM) specification for a long-range escort fighter. Three prototypes were built with DB600 engines, the first of these flying in May 1936.

COUNTRY OF ORIGIN: Germany

TYPE: (Bf 110C-4) two/three-seat heavy fighter

POWERPLANT: two 1100 hp (820 kW) Daimler-Benz DB 601A-1 12-cylinder inverted-Vee engines

PERFORMANCE: maximum speed 248 mph (560 km/h); climb to 19,685 ft (6000 m) in 10 minutes 12 seconds; service ceiling 32,810 ft (10,000 m); range 680 miles (1095 km)

WEIGHTS: empty 11,354 lb (5150 kg); maximum take-off 14,881 lb (6750 kg)

DIMENSIONS: span 53 ft 1.8 in (16.20 m); length 39 ft 8.33 in (12.1 m); height 13 ft 6.5 in (4.13 m) with the tail up

ARMAMENT: two .787 in (20 mm) fixed forward-firing cannon and four .312 in (7.92 mm) fixed forward-firing machine guns in the nose, and one .312 in (7.92 mm) trainable rearward-firing machine gun in the rear cockpit

Messerschmitt Bf 110s pictured over Athens during the Greek campaign of April 1940.

A heavy fighter that first flew in May 1936 and remained in production through World War II for a total of about 6000 aircraft, the Bf 110 entered service as the Bf 110B with two 700 hp (522 kW) Junkers Jumo 210 engines. Only 45 of Bf 110Bs aircraft were completed before the advent of the Bf 110C with two Daimler-Benz DB 601 engines. About 1300 of the Bf 110C-1 to C-3 fighter variants were built before production switched to the Bf 110C-4 to C-7 models with better protection and provision for the fighter-bomber and reconnaissance roles.

Vulnerable to lighter fighter aircraft

The Bf 110D, built in D-1 to D-3 variants, had greater fuel capacity (internal and external) for the long-range fighter, fighter-bomber and shipping escort roles, although some were later adapted as interim night-fighters, the type serving until a time early in 1943. The Bf 110 proved vulnerable during the Battle of Britain against smaller, lighter fighter aircraft. From autumn 1940 production of the indifferent Bf 110C/D was scaled down, but in the spring of 1941 two new variants appeared as the Bf 110E and Bf 110F. The Bf 110E was a relatively simple development of the Bf 110D with updated equipment, improved crew protection, a measure of structural strengthening, and racks under the outer wing panels for four 110 lb (50 kg) bombs as well as the standard pair of 500 kg (1102 lb) bombs under the fuselage. Bf 110E production stretched through the E-1 to E-3 variants.

A Messerschmitt Bf 110C of ZG26 "Horst Wessel," as it would have appeared in the summer of 1941.

Supermarine Spitfire

The prototype Spitfire, K5054, made its first flight on March 5, 1936, and, like the Hawker Hurricane with which it was to share so much fame, was powered by a Rolls-Royce Merlin "C" engine.

The Griffon-engined series of Spitfires, starting with the Mk XII, gave an enormous performance increase.

COUNTRY OF ORIGIN: United Kingdom

TYPE: (Spitfire Mk VA) single-seat fighter and fighter-bomber

POWERPLANT: one 1,478 hp (1102 kW) Rolls-Royce Merlin 45 12-cylinder Vee engine

PERFORMANCE: maximum speed 394 mph (594 km/h); initial climb rate 3950 ft (1204 m) per minute; service ceiling 36,500 ft (11,125 m); range 1,135 miles (1827 km)

WEIGHTS: empty 4998 lb (2267 kg); maximum take-off 6417 lb (2911 kg)

DIMENSIONS: span 36 ft 1 in (11.23 m); length 29 ft 11 in (9.12 m); height 9 ft 11 in (3.02 m)

ARMAMENT: eight .303 in (7.7 mm) fixed forward-firing machine guns in the leading edges of the wing

The first Spitfire Mk Is were delivered to No. 19 Squadron at Duxford in August 1938. Eight other squadrons had been equipped with Spitfires by September 1939, and two Auxiliary Air Force units, Nos. 603 and 609, were undergoing operational training. Production of the Spitfire Mk I reached 1566 aircraft. This variant saw the most combat in the Battle of Britain, the Mk II with the 1175 hp (8762 kW) Merlin XII engine being issued to the squadrons of Fighter Command in September 1940. The major Spitfire production version was the Mk V, with 6479 examples completed.

Pressurized cockpit

To counter the activities of high-flying German reconnaissance aircraft the Spitfire Mk VI was produced with a long, tapered wing and a pressurized cockpit; the aircraft was assigned to one flight of the RAF's home defense squadrons. The Mk VII, also with a pressurized cockpit, was powered by a Rolls-Royce Merlin 60 engine, a two-stage, two-speed, inter-cooled powerplant that was to

take development of the Merlin to its ultimate. Early in 1942, the Air Staff ordered a Mk V Spitfire airframe combined with a Merlin 61 engine. The result was the Spitfire Mk IX, which was a success. Deliveries to the RAF began in June 1942 and 5665 were built, more than any other mark except the Mk V. The Spitfire Mk X and XII were unarmed PR variants, while the Mk XII, powered by a 1735 hp (1294 kW) Rolls-Royce Griffon engine, was developed specifically to counter low-level attacks by Focke-Wulf 190s. Only 100 MK XII Spitfires were built, but they were followed by the Mk XIV. This was based on the Mk VIII, with an airframe strengthened to take a 2050 hp (1529 kW) Griffon 65 engine. The last variants of the Spitfire were the Mks 21, 22 and 24. They bore very little resemblance to the prototype Mk I of a decade earlier. Total production of the Spitfire was 20,351. The naval version was the Seafire.

This is a Spitfire Mk IIa of No. 74 Squadron, RAF Hornchurch, shown as it would have appeared in the summer of 1940.

Macchi MC.200 Saetta

The MC.200 Saetta (Lightning), the second of Italy's monoplane fighters, was designed by Mario Castoldi. He had been responsible for some very successful seaplane racers between the wars, such as the trophy-winning M.39.

COUNTRY OF ORIGIN: Italy

TYPE: (MC.200CB) single-seat fighter and fighter-bomber

POWERPLANT: one 870 hp (649 kW) Fiat A.74 RC.38 14-cylinder two-row radial engine

PERFORMANCE: maximum speed 312 mph (503 km/h); climb to 16,405 ft (5000 m) in 5 minutes 51 seconds; service ceiling 29,200 ft (8900 m); range 541 miles (870 km)

WEIGHTS: empty 4451 lb (2019 kg); normal take-off 5597 lb (2339 kg)

DIMENSIONS: span 34 ft 8.5 in (10.58 m); length 26 ft 10.4 in (8.19 m); height 11 ft 5.75 in (3.51 m)

ARMAMENT: two .5 in (12.7 mm) fixed forward-firing machine guns in the upper part of the forward fuselage, plus an external bomb load of 705 lb (320 kg)

One of the main handicaps suffered by the MC.200 was its bulky radial engine, which produced a lot of drag in combat.

The Saetta (Lightning) was one of the first generation of Italian low-wing monoplane fighters with advanced features such as retractable main landing-gear units, but like many of its contemporaries was limited in capability by a low-powered engine. Designed from 1936 and first flown in prototype form during December 1937, the MC.200 entered service in October 1939.

Escort fighter and fighter bomber

The original type of enclosed cockpit was initially altered to an open and finally a semi-enclosed type ostensibly because of Italian pilot preference. Production totalled 1150 aircraft, later aircraft having the outer wings of the MC.202 with two .303 in (7.7 mm) machine guns. With the advent of the more capable MC.202, the MC.200 was relegated to the escort fighter and fighter-bomber roles (MC.200CB), and the MC.20AS was a tropicalized type for North African service. The MC.200 was followed by the much more effective MC.202, with a Daimler-Benz DB.601 in-line engine. The type entered service with the 1st Stormo at Udine in the summer of 1941, moving to Sicily to take part in operations over Malta in November. The Folgore remained in production until the Italian armistice of September 1943, although the rate of production was always influenced by the availability of engines. Macchi built 392 MC.202s, and around 1100 more were produced by other companies, mainly Breda.

Seen here is a Macchi MC.202 of the 90th Squadriglia, Regia Aeronautica, Western Desert 1941.

Curtiss P-40

The P-40 originated as a development of the radial-engined Curtiss P-36A Hawk. The prototype XP-40, which flew for the first time in October 1938, was praised for its handling characteristics by USAAC test pilots.

COUNTRY OF ORIGIN: USA

TYPE: (P-40M) single-seat fighter and fighter-bomber

POWERPLANT: one 1200 hp (895 kW) Allison V-1710-81 12-cylinder Vee engine

PERFORMANCE: maximum speed 343 mph (552 km/h); climb to 20,000 ft (6095 m) in 8 minutes 48 seconds; service ceiling 31,000 ft (9450 m); range 750 miles (1207 km)

WEIGHTS: empty 6200 lb (2812 kg); maximum take-off 11,400 lb (5171 kg)

DIMENSIONS: span 37 ft 3.5 in (11.37 m); length 33 ft 4 in (10.16 m); height 10 ft 7 in (3.23 m)

ARMAMENT: six .5 in (12.7 mm) fixed forward-firing machine guns in the leading edges of the wing, plus an external bomb load of 1500 lb (680 kg)

The Curtiss P-40 was not an ideal type in fighter-versus-fighter combat, but it proved its worth as a fighter-bomber.

The R-1830 engine was reliable and powerful by the standards of the 1930s, but when it became clear that it lacked the potential for development into more powerful forms, full exploitation of the Model 75 airframe was schemed on the basis of the Allison V-1710 Vee engine. The installation of this engine into a converted P-36A created the Model 81 that first flew in October 1938 as the XP-40.

First production model
The first production model was the P-40 of which 199 were delivered with the 1150 hp (976 kW) V-1710-33 engine for service from May 1940. There followed 131, 193, 22 and 2320 examples of the P-40B, P-40C, P-40D

and P-40E as well as 2060 Tomahawk Mk Is for the UK. The P-40 was an adequate fighter by the standards of early World War II, but really made its mark as a capable fighter-bomber in the close support role. Further development of the Model 81 resulted in the Model 87, with a Packard V-1650 (Rolls-Royce Merlin) engine. The XP-40F prototype conversion and the three YP-40F service test aircraft paved the way for 1311 P-40F fighter-bombers. Other main variants included the P-40K version of the P-40F with the V-1710-73 engine (1300 aircraft), P-40L with two wing guns removed (700), P-40M with the V-1710-81 engine (600), P-40N (a lightened version of the P-40L/M – 5219 built) and finally the P-40R re-engined conversions of 300 P-40F/L aircraft.

The RAF used the P-40 as the Kittyhawk. Seen here is an aircraft of No. 112 Squadron, Desert Air Force.

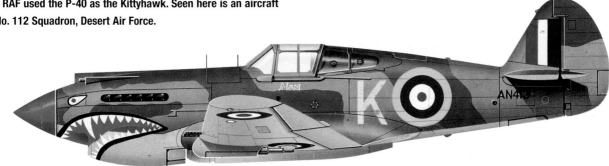

Fiat CR.42 Falco

The age of the monoplane had dawned, yet Fiat's Celestino Rosatelli persisted with the open-cockpit, fabric-covered fighter biplane concept and developed the Fiat CR.41, a variant of the CR.32 with a radial engine.

The Fiat CR.42 was a nimble and effective fighter, and was a worthy opponent for the RAF's Gloster Gladiator.

COUNTRY OF ORIGIN: Italy

TYPE: (CR.42) single-seat fighter

POWERPLANT: one 840 hp (626 kW) Fiat A.74 R1C.38 14-cylinder, two-row radial engine

PERFORMANCE: maximum speed 293 mph (472 km/h); climb to 16,405 ft (6000 m) in 7 minutes 30 seconds; service ceiling 32,265 ft (9835 m); range 416 miles (670 km)

WEIGHTS: empty 4354 lb (1975 kg); maximum take-off 5324 lb (2415 kg)

DIMENSIONS: span 35 ft 11.5 in (10.96 m); length 25 ft 6.75 in (7.79 m); height 9 ft 8 in (2.96 m)

ARMAMENT: two .5 in (12.7 mm) Breda-SAFAT fixed forward-firing machine guns in the upper part of the forward fuselage

By the mid-1930s most of Rosatelli's contemporaries had started designing stressed-skin monoplanes, but the Fiat Chief Engineer persisted with the open-cockpit, fabric-covered CR family and developed the CR.41, a variant of the CR.32 with 900 hp (671 kW) Gnome-Rhône radial engine and modified tail surfaces.

Horrendous losses

From this stemmed the CR.42. This was a robust, clean and attractive aircraft, but was obsolete by its first flight in 1936. Yet the CR.42 found a ready market and went into large-scale production for the Regia Aeronautica and for Belgium, Hungary and Sweden. A group of 50 CR.42bis aircraft were stationed in Belgium from October 1940 to January 1941 under the command of Luftflotte II, but these suffered such horrendous losses at the hands of RAF pilots they were redeployed to North Africa. When the situation became untenable there, the survivors were flown to Italy in readiness for the invasion of June 1943. During the autumn and early winter Allied forces advanced steadily forward to the Gothic line with a vast air armada. With their own stocks running low, the Germans followed the Russians' example and pressed any available aircraft into service for night nuisance attacks.

This is one of the CR.42s that served in North Africa with 97a Squadriglia. The unit was based at Benina in Libya during 1940.

Brewster F2A and Buffalo

The RAF rejected the F2A Buffalo for operational service in Europe, but deemed it suitable for service in the Far East, where it was hopelessly outclassed by Japanese fighters in Malaya, Singapore and Burma.

COUNTRY OF ORIGIN: USA

TYPE: (F2A-3) single-seat carrierborne and land-based fighter/fighter-bomber

POWERPLANT: one 1200 hp (895 kW) Wright R–1820-40 Cyclone nine-cylinder single-row radial engine

PERFORMANCE: maximum speed 321 mph (517 km/h); initial climb rate 2290 ft (698 m) per minute; service ceiling 33,200 ft (10,120 m); range 1680 miles (2704 km)

WEIGHTS: empty 4732 lb (2146 kg); normal take-off 6321 lb (2867 kg); maximum take-off 7159 lb (3247 kg)

DIMENSIONS: span 35 ft (10.67 m); length 26 ft 4 in (8.03 m); height 12 ft 1 in (3.68 m)

ARMAMENT: two .5 in (12.7 mm) fixed forward-firing machine guns in upper part of the forward fuselage; two .5 in (12.7 mm) fixed forward-firing machine guns in the leading edges of the wing, plus a bomb load of 232 lb (105 kg)

The Buffalo had many shortcomings, but was well liked by Finnish pilots who called it the "Sky Pearl."

Ordered as the US Navy's first monoplane fighter, the F2A first flew in XF2A-1 prototype form in January 1938 and paved the way for 11 F2A-1 production aircraft that entered service in July 1939 with the 940 hp (701 kW) R-1820-34 engine, then 43 and 108 examples of the F2A-2 and F2A-3, the former with an uprated engine and the latter with more armor and a longer nose. The F2A was largely unsuccessful in US service. It was also ordered in B-239 (44 for Finland, which was the sole country to operate the type with major success), B-339B (40 for Belgium of which 38 were delivered to the UK as Buffalo Mk Is), B-339D (72 for the Netherlands East Indies), B-339E (170 for the UK as Buffalo Mk Is), and B-439 (20 for the Netherlands East Indies but all impressed by the US Army that later delivered 17 to Australia) form.

Success for the Finns

In Finnish service the Buffalo performed well, serving in what the Finns called the "Continuation War," in which Finland fought on Germany's side after the invasion of the USSR in 1941. Its leading exponent was Warrant Officer Ilmari Juutilainen, who shot down 36 Russian aircraft. He continued to fly the Buffalo until 1943, when he converted to Messerschmitt 109s, and gained 94 victories.

A Brewster F2A in the US Army Air Corps markings adopted early in 1942. The red has been deleted from the national insignia to avoid confusion with the Japanese "Hinomaru."

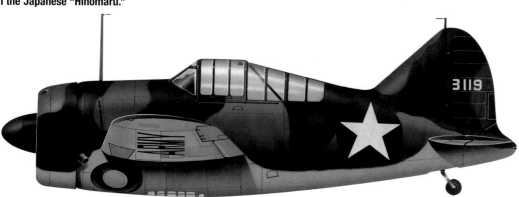

Dewoitine D.520

The D.520 was without doubt the best of France's home-produced fighters at the time of the German invasion in May 1940. It originated as a private venture, and the first prototype flew on October 2, 1938.

COUNTRY OF ORIGIN: France

TYPE: (D.520C.1) single-seat fighter

POWERPLANT: one 930 hp (693 kW) Hispano-Suiza 12Y-45 12-cylinder Vee engine

PERFORMANCE: maximum speed 336 mph (540 km/h); climb to 13,125 ft (4000 m) in 5 minutes 49 seconds; service ceiling 36,090 ft (11,000 m); range 957 miles (1540 km)

WEIGHTS: empty 4685 lb (2125 kg); maximum take-off 6151 lb (2790 kg)

DIMENSIONS: span 33 ft 5.5 in (10.20 m); length 28 ft 8.75 in (8.76 m); height 8ft 5.25 in (2.57 m)

ARMAMENT: one .787 in (20 mm) fixed forward-firing cannon in the nose, and four .295 in (7.5 mm) fixed forward-firing machine guns in the leading edges of the wing

The Dewoitine D.520 was a very elegant aircraft, its clean lines apparent in this photograph.

The D.520 resulted from a 1934 requirement for an advanced single-seat fighter to replace types such as the Dewoitine D.510, which had been rendered obsolete. The aircraft was developed via the indifferent D.513 to meet a revised 1936 requirement, and incorporated features such as cantilever low-set flapped wing, enclosed cockpit, landing gear with retractable main units and engine delivering 1000 hp (746 kW) driving a variable-pitch propeller.

First flight

The D.520 prototype first flew in October 1938, and only 36 D.520C.1 fighters had been delivered before the German invasion of May 1940. Further deliveries were made during the German offensive, and the D.520 acquitted itself very well. Production eventually reached 905 aircraft for service, mainly with the Vichy French Air Force, and were also passed to Germany's allies. During the Battle of France the D.520 was operational with GC I/3. Four more groupes de chasse and three naval escadrilles re-armed with the type before France's surrender, but only GC I/3, II/7, II/6 and the naval AC 1 saw any action. The D.520 groupes claimed 114 victories and 39 probables; 85 D.520s were lost. The D.520 also saw action against the Allies during the invasion of Syria in June 1941, its main opponent being the Hawker Hurricane.

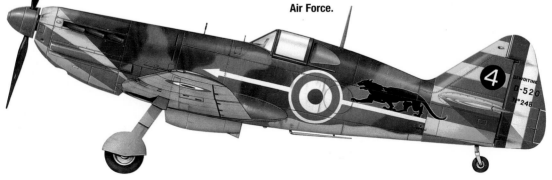

This a Dewoitine D.520 wearing the markings of the Vichy French Air Force.

Bell P-39 Airacobra

Although the Western Allies did not rate the P-39 Airacobra very highly, the Russians used it with great success, and some of their leading air aces gained many victories while flying it.

COUNTRY OF ORIGIN: USA

TYPE: (P-39N) single-seat fighter and fighter-bomber

POWERPLANT: one 1125 hp (839 kW) Allison V-1710-85 12-cylinder Vee engine

PERFORMANCE: maximum speed 376 mph (605 km/h); climb to 15,000 ft (4570 m) in 6 minutes 6 seconds; service ceiling 38,270 ft (11,665 m); range 975 miles (1569 km)

WEIGHTS: empty 6400 lb (2903 kg); maximum take-off 8800 lb (3992 kg)

DIMENSIONS: span 34 ft (10.36 m); length 30 ft 2 in (9.2 m); height 12 ft 5 in (3.79 m)

ARMAMENT: one 1.46 in (37 mm) fixed forward-firing cannon and two .5 in (12.7 mm) fixed forward-firing machine guns in the nose, and four .3 in (7.62 mm) fixed forward-firing machine guns in the leading edges of the wing, plus an external bomb load of 500 lb (227 kg)

These P-39 Airacobras are training aircraft, as denoted by the large codes on their noses.

The P-39 was a bold attempt to create an advanced fighter by locating the engine in the fuselage behind the cockpit, from where it drove the tractor propeller by means of a long extension shaft. This was meant to leave the nose free for a concentrated forward-firing battery of guns, improve agility by locating the engine nearer the center of gravity, and facilitate the use of tricycle landing gear.

Ground-attack role

The XP-39 prototype first flew in April 1938, and a number of prototype and pre-production standards appeared before the P-39D entered service as the first operational model. It served with 13 groups, yet the US Army never deemed the P-39 successful, and 4924 of the 9590 aircraft were shipped to the USSR for use mainly in the ground-attack role. The other main variants were the P-39F, J, K, L, M, N and Q. In US service, the Airacobra went into action with the 8th Pursuit Group in northern Australia early in 1942, subsequently deploying its aircraft to forward airstrips in New Guinea. Later the unit's designation was changed to the 8th Fighter Group and it was joined by the 35th Fighter Group, also with P-39s. The fighters were a mixture of P-39Ds and Airacobra Mk Is, drawn from the cancelled UK order. P-39s were also used by the 347th Fighter Group in New Caledonia, with detachments sent to Guadalcanal for air defense. As well as the Pacific, P-39s saw action during the invasion of southern France, and were used by Free French squadrons.

Many P-39s were supplied to the Soviet Union, where the type was generally well liked by its pilots.

Grumman F4F Wildcat

In March 1936, the Grumman Aircraft Corporation won a contract to build an all-metal biplane fighter, the XF4F-1, for the US Navy. But the biplane configuration was quickly shelved in favor of a monoplane design, the XF4F-2.

COUNTRY OF ORIGIN: USA

TYPE: (F4F-4 and Wildcat Mk II) single-seat carrierborne fighter and fighter-bomber

POWERPLANT: one 1200 hp (895 kW) Pratt & Whitney R-1830-86 Twin Wasp 14-cylinder two-row radial engine

PERFORMANCE: maximum speed 318 mph (512 km/h); initial climb rate 1950 ft (594 m) per minute; service ceiling 34,000 ft (10,365 m); range 1250 miles (2012 km)

WEIGHTS: empty 5758 lb (2612 kg); maximum take-off 7952 lb (3607 kg)

DIMENSIONS: span 38 ft (11.58 m); length 28 ft 9 in (8.76 m); height 9 ft 2.5 in (2.81 m)

ARMAMENT: six .5 in (12.7 mm) fixed forward-firing machine guns in the leading edges of the wing, plus an external bomb load of 200 lb (91 kg)

The US Navy decided to develop the aircraft still further by installing a supercharged XR-1830-76 engine in a much redesigned airframe, the revamped machine, designated XF4F-3, flying for the first time on February 12, 1939. In August, the Navy issued its first production contract for 53 Grumman F4F-3 Wildcats, as the fighter had been named. The first production aircraft flew in February 1940, but deliveries were slow and by the end of 1940 only 22 Wildcats had been handed over to Navy fighter squadrons VF-4 and VF-7, these units embarking on the USS *Ranger* and USS *Wasp* respectively.

This F4F saw action over Guadalcanal, where it was flown by US Marine Corps ace and Medal of Honor winner Captain Joe Foss.

Only an experienced pilot could give the Wildcat a chance of survival in combat with Japanese fighters.

Replacing all other carrierborne fighters

In 1939 France expressed an interest in acquiring 100 Wildcats. When France was overrun, the order was taken over by the British Purchasing Commission on behalf of the Royal Navy, who designated it the F4F-3 the Martlet I. The first was delivered on July 27, 1940. In October No. 804 Squadron began re-arming with the Martlet at Hatson, in the Orkney Islands, and scored an early success when two of its aircraft shot down a Junkers Ju 88 over the naval base at Scapa Flow. The total number of Martlets of all marks supplied to Britain reached 1191. In US service, the Wildcat with folding wings received the designation F4F-4, the first example going to fighter squadron VF-42 in May for trials on the USS *Yorktown*. As 1941 drew to a close the Wildcat was rapidly replacing all other US carrierborne fighters. As the American pilots gained combat experience during 1942, their superior tactics and teamwork began to have a telling effect on the course of the Pacific air war. In US Marine Corps hands, the Wildcat will forever be remembered for its defense of Guadalcanal in the latter half of 1942. In total 7885 Wildcats were built.

Nakajima Ki-43 Hayabusa "Oscar"

Like its naval counterpart, the Mitsubishi Zero, the Nakajima Ki-43 Hayabusa (Peregrine Falcon) was in action from the first day of Japan's war until the last, by which time it was outclassed by the latest Allied fighters.

COUNTRY OF ORIGIN: Japan

TYPE: (Ki-43-IIb) single-seat fighter and fighter-bomber

POWERPLANT: one 1150 hp (857 kW) Nakajima Ha-115 (Army Type 1) 14-cylinder two-row radial engine

PERFORMANCE: maximum speed 329 mph (530 km/h); climb to 16,405 ft (5000 m) in 5 minutes 49 seconds; service ceiling 36,750 ft (11,200 m); range 1988 miles (3200 km)

WEIGHTS: empty 4211 lb (1910 kg); normal take-off 5710 lb (2590 kg); maximum take-off 6450 lb (2925 kg)

DIMENSIONS: span 35 ft 6.75 in (10.84 m); length 29 ft 3.25 in (8.92 m); height 10 ft 8.75 in (3.27 m)

ARMAMENT: two .5 in (12.7 mm) fixed forward-firing machine guns in the upper part of the forward fuselage, plus an external bomb load of 1102 lb (500 kg)

Although not as effective as its naval counterpart, the Zero, the Ki-43 Hayabusa gave good service to the Japanese Army Air Force.

The Ki-43 Hayabusa ("Peregrine Falcon") was the most advanced fighter available to the Imperial Japanese Army Air Force in the opening phases of World War II, and as such the type came as a huge shock to the Allied air forces.

Excellent and versatile fighter

It was also the most important of all the Imperial Japanese Army Air Force's fighters numerically, with more than 5900 aircraft built right up to the end of the war, by which time it was obsolete in terms of firepower and protection. The main variants were the Ki-43-I (three subvariants) with the 980 hp (731 kW) Ha-25 engine driving a two-blade propeller, Ki-43-II (three subvariants) with an uprated engine driving a three-blade propeller, and the Ki-43-III (one subvariant) with the 1230 hp (917 kW) Ha-115-II engine. The Hayabusa was the Allies' main opponent in Burma and was encountered in numbers during the battle for Leyte, in the Philippines, and in the defense of the Kurile Islands. An excellent, versatile fighter, its main drawback was a lack of adequate armament. Its Army pilots were less skillful than their Japanese Navy counterparts, and suffered accordingly.

This is a Ki-43IIb of the 3rd Chutai, 25th Sentai, Imperial Japanese Army Air Force, as it looked when it was based at Hankow in China, in January 1944.

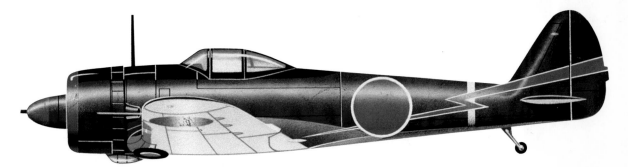

Focke-Wulf Fw 190

The Focke-Wulf Fw 190 stemmed from a suggestion by the German Air Ministry in 1937 that the company should develop an interceptor fighter to complement the Bf 109. The result was a truly formidable fighter.

COUNTRY OF ORIGIN: Germany

TYPE: (Fw 190F-3) single-seat ground-attack and close-support fighter

POWERPLANT: one 1700 hp (1267.5 kW) BMW 801D-2 14-cylinder two-row radial engine

PERFORMANCE: maximum speed 395 mph (635 km/h); initial climb rate 2106 ft (642 m) per minute; service ceiling 34,780 ft (10,600 m); range 466 miles (750 km)

WEIGHTS: empty 7328 lb (3325 kg); maximum take-off 10,858 lb (4925 kg)

DIMENSIONS: span 34 ft 5.5 in (10.5 m); length 29 ft 4.25 in (8.95 m); height 12 ft 11.5 in (3.95 m)

ARMAMENT: two .787 in (20 mm) fixed forward-firing cannons in the wing roots and two .512 in (13 mm) fixed forward-firing machine guns in the upper part of the forward fuselage, plus an external bomb load of 2646 lb (1200 kg)

Nicknamed the "Butcher Bird," the Fw 190 was superior to any Allied fighter type when it first appeared in 1941.

The Fw 190 was the only German fighter to enter service and large-scale production during the course of the war. It was developed to a definitive standard as the Fw 190D with a Vee engine. The first Fw 190 prototype flew in June 1939 and, after intensive development concentrated on the alternative BMW 139 or BMW 801 engines and a shorter- or longer-span wing, the Fw 190A entered production with the BMW 801 and larger wing. The 40 Fw 190A-0 pre-production aircraft were followed by 100 Fw 190A-1 fighters, and the type entered service in the autumn of 1941. There followed 426 longer-span Fw 190A-2 fighters with heavier armament, 509 Fw 190A-3 fighter-bombers with revised armament, and 894 Fw 190A-4 fighter-bombers with a methanol/water power boost system.

Adapted for other roles

The Fw 190 was so adaptable it was developed as the Fw 190F series for the dedicated ground-attack role. Entering service at the end of 1942, the Fw 190F-1 (about 30 aircraft) was the production-line version of the Fw 190A-5/U3 fighter based on the Fw 190A-4 with strengthened landing gear, more armor protection, and a combination of one ETC 501 bomb rack under the fuselage and four ETC 50 bomb racks under the wings.

This is a Focke-Wulf Fw 190A-3 of JG2, France, 1942. Its tail shows nineteen victory markings.

Bristol Beaufighter

In October 1938, the Bristol Aeroplane Company submitted a proposal for a twin-engined night-fighter, heavily armed and equipped with AI radar, to the RAF Air Staff. It was originally called the Beaufort Fighter.

COUNTRY OF ORIGIN: United Kingdom

TYPE: (Beaufighter Mk VIF) two-seat night-fighter

POWERPLANT: two 1635 hp (1219 kW) Bristol Hercules VI 14-cylinder two-row radial engines

PERFORMANCE: maximum speed 33 3mph (536 km/h); initial climb rate not available; service ceiling not available; range 1540 miles (2478 km)

WEIGHTS: empty 14,600 lb (6622 kg); maximum take-off 21,600 lb (9798 kg)

DIMENSIONS: span 57 ft 10 in (17.63 m); length 41 ft 8 in (12.70 m); height 15 ft 10 in (4.82 m)

ARMAMENT: four .787 in (20 mm) fixed forward-firing cannons in the underside of the forward fuselage, and six .303 in (7.7 mm) fixed forward-firing machine guns in the leading edges of the wing (two to port and four to starboard)

Beaufighter Mk X aircraft of No. 404 Coastal Command Squadron break into the circuit at RAF Dallachy, Scotland, early 1945.

The Beaufighter was a derivative of the Beaufort torpedo bomber and was first flown in July 1939 as a heavy fighter with a smaller fuselage and an uprated powerplant of two 1400 hp (1044 kW) Bristol Hercules III or 1500 hp (1118 kW) Hercules XI radial engines. Some 553 Mk IF radar-equipped night-fighters and 397 Mk IC coastal fighters were fitted with Hercules engines and were later complemented by 597 Mk IIF night-fighters with 1280 hp (954 kW) Rolls-Royce Merlin XX Vee engines.

Heavy armament provides a bigger punch

It came into its own during 1942 in its Mk VI form. There were three subvariants: the Beaufighter Mk VIC torpedo fighter (693 aircraft); the Beaufighter Mk VIF night-fighter (879 aircraft); and the Beaufighter Mk VI Interim Torpedo Fighter (60 aircraft) with underwing provision for eight 60 lb (27 kg) rockets. The Beaufighter TF.Mk X was an improved version of the Beaufighter Mk VIC with Hercules XVII engines optimized for low rather than medium altitude as required for anti-shipping operations. Production of the Beaufighter TF.Mk X, which was the most important British anti-ship attack weapon from 1944 in Europe and the Far East, totalled 2205 aircraft, and another 163 machines were completed to the Beaufighter Mk XIC standard that differed from the Beaufighter TF.Mk X only in possessing no torpedo capability.

This aircraft is a Mk VIF, serving with the 416th Night Fighter Squadron, USAAF.

Lockheed P-38 Lightning

It tended to be overshadowed by the Republic P-47 Thunderbolt and the North American P-51 Mustang, but the Lockheed P-38 Lightning played a vital part in winning air superiority for the Allies, particularly in the Pacific.

An early model P-38 on a test flight from the Lockheed factory at Burbank, California.

COUNTRY OF ORIGIN: USA

TYPE: (P-38L) single-seat long-range fighter and fighter-bomber

POWERPLANT: two 1600 hp (1193 kW) Allison V-1710-111/113 (F30) 12-cylinder Vee engines

PERFORMANCE: maximum speed 414 mph (666 km/h); climb to 20,000 ft (6095 m) in 7 minutes; service ceiling 44,000 ft (13,410 m); range 2600 miles (4184 km)

WEIGHTS: empty 12,800 lb (5806 kg); maximum take-off 21,600 lb (9798 kg)

DIMENSIONS: span 52 ft (15.85 m); length 37 ft 10 in (11.53 m); height 12 ft 10 in (3.91 m)

ARMAMENT: one .787 in (20 mm) fixed forward-firing cannon and four .5 in (12.7 mm) fixed forward-firing machine guns in the nose, plus an external bomb and rocket load of 4000 lb (1814 kg)

The P-38A heavy fighter had its empennage carried by two booms supporting the main units of the tricycle landing gear as well as the two engines' turbochargers. The pilot sat in the central nacelle behind heavy nose armament and nosewheel unit. The XP-38 prototype first flew in January 1939, and considerable development paved the way for the P-38D initial operational variant (36 aircraft) that entered service in August 1941.

Replacing all other carrierborne fighters
Total production was 9393 aircraft including conversions to F-4 and F-5 reconnaissance standards. The most important fighter variants were the P-38E (210), P-38F (527), P-38G (1082), P-38H (601), P-38J (2970) and P-38L (3923). The type served successfully in every US theater. One of the most famous operations carried out by the Lightning was on April 18, 1943, when P-38s of the 339th Fighter Squadron, USAAF, shot down a Japanese bomber carrying Admiral Isoroku Yamamoto, the Japanese Navy Commander-in-Chief. To do the job, the Lightnings made a 1100-mile (1770km) round trip from Guadalcanal to intercept Yamamoto's aircraft over Kahili Atoll. The two top-scoring pilots of the Pacific war, Major Richard I Bong and Major Tommy McGuire, both flew P-38s.

This is a Lockheed P-38 Lightning of the 55th Fighter Squadron, 20th Fighter Group, King's Cliffe, England, 1944.

Mitsubishi A6M Reisen "Zero"

One of the finest aircraft of all time, the Mitsubishi A6M Reisen (Zero fighter) first flew on April 1, 1939, powered by a 780 hp Zuisei 13 radial engine. It was accepted for service with the Japanese Naval Air Force in July 1940.

COUNTRY OF ORIGIN: Japan

TYPE: (A6M2 Model 21) single-seat carrierborne and land-based fighter and fighter-bomber

POWERPLANT: one 950 hp (708 kW) Nakajima NK1C Sakae 12 14-cylinder two-row radial engine

PERFORMANCE: maximum speed 332 mph (534 km/h); climb to 19,685 ft (6000 m) in 7 minutes 27 seconds; service ceiling 32,810 ft (10,000 m); range 1929 miles (3104 km)

WEIGHTS: empty 3704 lb (1680 kg); maximum take-off 6164 lb (2796 kg)

DIMENSIONS: span 39 ft 4.5 in (12 m); length 29 ft 8.75 in (9.06 m); height 10 ft (3.05 m)

ARMAMENT: two .787 in (20 mm) fixed forward-firing cannons in the leading edges of the wing, and two .303 in (7.7 mm) fixed forward-firing machine guns in the forward fuselage, plus an external bomb load of 265 lb (120 kg)

Mitsubishi A6M2 Zero of the 12th Air Group, seen over China shortly after the type's entry into service in 1940.

The A6M was generally known in the West as the Zero. The A6M rightly remains the most famous of all Japanese warplanes of World War II and in its heyday was a superb naval fighter. It is also important as the first carrierborne fighter anywhere in the world to achieve full parity with the best of its land-based contemporaries but for lack of an adequate successor was maintained in development and production (11,280 aircraft) past its effective limits. The type reached its apogee as a dogfighting warplane in the

A6M2, while the A6M3 had greater power but shorter range, the A6M5 heavier firepower, and the A6M6 better protection and greater fighter-bomber capability.

Impressive combat record

When fitted with a drop tank the Zero had phenomenal range. In 1942 the Americans allocated the code-name Zeke to the A6M, but as time went by the name Zero came into general use. During the first months of the Pacific war the Zeros carved out an impressive combat record. In the battle for Java, which ended on March 8, 1942, they destroyed 550 Allied aircraft. These remarkable victories earned enormous prestige for the Japanese Navy pilots and tended to overshadow the achievements of their Army colleagues, who fought no less tenaciously albeit with less spectacular success. Throughout the war, the demands of the Navy were to receive priority.

Instead of being built in several separate units, the Zero was constructed in two pieces.

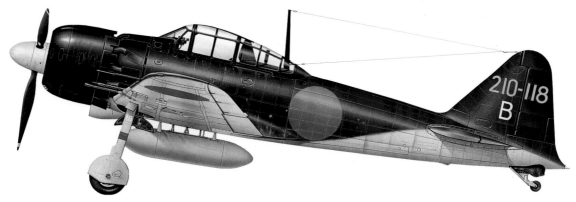

de Havilland Mosquito F.Mk.II

The all-wood de Havilland DH.98 Mosquito was one of the most versatile and successful aircraft of World War II. In March 1940 the Air Ministry issued Specification B.1/40, and the first prototype flew on November 25, 1940.

COUNTRY OF ORIGIN: United Kingdom

TYPE: two-seat night-fighter

POWERPLANT: two 1480 hp (1103.6 kW) Rolls-Royce Merlin 21 12-cylinder Vee-type engines

PERFORMANCE: maximum speed 370 mph (595 km/h)

WEIGHTS: empty 14,300 lb (6492 kg); max. take-off 20,000 lb (9072 kg)

DIMENSIONS: span 54 ft 2 in (16.51 m); length 42 ft 11 in (13.08 m); height 17 ft 5 in (5.31 m)

ARMAMENT: four .787 in (20 mm) Hispano cannonc and four .303 in (7.7 mm) Browning machine guns in nose

With the night-fighter versions of the Mosquito, the RAF at last had an effective means of dealing with German night intruders.

The PR Mosquito was the first into service, issued to No. 1 Photographic Reconnaissance Unit at RAF Benson in 1941. The first Mosquito B.IV bombers went to No. 105 Squadron in 1942. Total production of the B.IV was 273 aircraft. The Mosquito night-fighter prototype was completed with AI Mk IV radar in a "solid" nose and a powerful armament of four .787 in (20 mm) cannons and four machine guns. The first Mosquito fighter squadron, No. 157, formed at Debden in Essex on December 13, 1941. Ninety-seven Mk II night-fighters were later converted to NF.Mk.XII standard. They were followed by 270 NF.Mk.XIIIs, the production counterpart of the Mk.XII. These and subsequent night-fighter Mosquitoes retained only the .787 in (20 mm) cannon armament.

Seen here is an early production Mosquito NF.Mk.II in the markings of No. 157 Squadron, Castle Camps, Essex, mid-1942.

Low-level precision attackers

Other specialist night-fighter Mosquitoes were the Mks XV and XVII, 100 of which were converted from Mk IIs, and the NF.Mk.XIX. The major Mosquito production version, the FB.Mk.VI, first flew in February 1943. The aircraft could carry two 250 or 500 lb (113 or 227 kg) bombs in the rear of the bomb bay, with two additional bombs or auxiliary fuel tanks. The Mosquito Mk VI entered service with No. 418 Squadron in 1943 and subsequently armed several squadrons of No. 2 Group. These squadrons carried out some daring low-level precision attacks late in the war, including the raid on Amiens prison in February 1944 and attacks on Gestapo headquarters buildings.

Chance Vought F4U Corsair

The F4U Corsair became operational with Navy Fighting Squadron VF-17 in April 1943. As pilots became experienced in flying their powerful new fighter-bombers they became formidable opponents.

COUNTRY OF ORIGIN: USA

TYPE: (F4U-1A) single-seat shipborne and land-based fighter

POWERPLANT: one 2,000 hp (1491 kW) Pratt & Whitney R-2800-8 Double Wasp radial engine

PERFORMANCE: maximum speed 417 mph (671 km/h); climb to 3,120 ft (951 m) in 1 minute; service ceiling 36,900 ft (11,245 m); range 1015 miles (1633 km)

WEIGHTS: empty 8982 lb (4074 kg); maximum take-off 14,000 lb (6350 kg)

DIMENSIONS: span 41 ft (12.5 m); length 33 ft 4 in (10.16 m); height 16 ft 1 in (4.9 m)

ARMAMENT: six .5 in (12.7 mm) fixed forward-firing machine guns in the leading edge of the wing

An F4U Corsair runs up its powerful Pratt & Whitney radial engine prior to a sortie.

This is an F4U Corsair of Fleet Composite Squadron VC-3, which flew night-fighter operations in Korea.

Development of the V-166B began in 1938, with the aim of tailoring the smallest possible airframe to fit the powerful Pratt & Whitney XR-2800 Double Wasp engine. The highly cranked wing was designed to allow clearance for the large-diameter propeller, without the need for overlong main gear units. The XF4U-1 prototype first flew in May 1940, but it was not until the following February that the US Navy placed an order for 585 F4U-1 production aircraft. Carrier evaluation proved disappointing, leading to changes in the landing gear and cockpit height to improve forward view. Most aircraft were modified on the production line and were designated F4U-1A. Initial operational service was with the USMC (February 1943), but the aircraft later distinguished itself with both the US Navy and Fleet Air Arm. Of the 12,681 Corsairs built during WWII, 2012 were supplied to the Royal Navy, equipping 19 squadrons of the Fleet Air Arm; some of these aircraft were diverted to equip three squadrons of the Royal New Zealand Air Force, operating in the Solomons. Variants of the Corsair included the F4U-1C cannon-armed fighter, F4U-1D fighter-bomber, F4U-2 night-fighter, F4U-3 high-altitude research version, and F4U-4 fighter. Post-war developments included the F4U-5 fighter-bomber, F4U-5N night-fighter and F4U-5P photo reconnaissance aircraft, the F4U-6 (later A-1) attack aircraft and the F4U-7, also supplied to the French Navy. French Corsairs saw combat during the Anglo-French Suez operation of 1956.

North American P-51 Mustang

The North American P-51 Mustang was produced in response to a 1940 RAF requirement for a fast, heavily armed fighter to operate at altitudes above 20,000 ft (6100 m). North American built the prototype in 117 days.

This photograph shows a P-51B of the 354th Squadron, 355th Fighter Group, Steeple Morden, England, 1944.

COUNTRY OF ORIGIN: USA

TYPE: (P-51D) single-seat fighter and fighter-bomber

POWERPLANT: one 1695 hp (1264 kW) Packard V-1650-7 12-cylinder Vee engine

PERFORMANCE: maximum speed 437 mph (703 km/h); climb to 20,000 ft (6095 m) in 7 minutes 18 seconds; service ceiling 41,900 ft (12,770 m); range 2301 miles (3703 km)

WEIGHTS: empty 6840 lb (3103 kg); maximum take-off 12,100 lb (5493 kg)

DIMENSIONS: span 37 ft .25 in (11.28 m); length 32 ft 3.25 in (9.84 m); height 13 ft 8 in (4.16 m) with the tail down

ARMAMENT: six .5 in (12.7 mm) fixed forward-firing machine guns in the leading edges of the wing, plus an external bomb and rocket load of 2000 lb (907 kg)

The Mustang was the finest all-around fighter of World War II. A superb warplane, it had phenomenal performance, good acceleration, very good maneuverability, an extremely sturdy airframe and other operationally significant attributes, all in an attractive package.

Mustang airframe and Merlin engine

The Mustang resulted from a British requirement and first flew in October 1940 with the Allison V-1710 engine, which was also used in the 1045 examples of the P-51 and P-51A (Mustang Mks I and II) that served from April 1942. The P-51B and P-51C (1988 and 1750 aircraft respectively) then switched to the Packard V-1650 American-made version of a classic British engine, the Rolls-Royce Merlin. This transformed the Mustang from a mediocre aircraft into one of the most important fighters of World War II. The combination of the Mustang airframe and Merlin engine had proved ideal in the P-51B/C and paved the way for most later developments. The first of these was the definitive P-51D, of which 7966 were completed with a cut-down rear fuselage and clear-view bubble canopy, and later with increased fuel capacity and underwing provision for rocket projectiles as alternatives to bombs for the increasingly important ground-attack role. The P-51D was one of the decisive weapons of World War II, and was complemented by the P-51H lightweight model (555 aircraft) and the P-51K version of the P-51D with a different propeller (1337 aircraft).

This is a P-51D Mustang of the 352nd Fighter Squadron, 353rd Fighter Group, Raydon, England, 1944.

Hawker Typhoon

The Hawker Typhoon found its place in history as the most potent Allied fighter-bomber of all. After the Allied landings in Normandy, the name of the rocket-armed Typhoon became synonymous with the break-up of an enemy armored counter-attack at Mortain and the destruction of the retreating German army at Falaise.

COUNTRY OF ORIGIN: United Kingdom

TYPE: (Mk 1A) single-seat interceptor

POWERPLANT: one 2100 hp (1566 kW) Napier Sabre I 24-cylinder H-type engine

PERFORMANCE: maximum speed about 412 mph (663km/h); climb to 15,000 ft (4570 m) in 5 minutes 50 seconds; service ceiling 35,200 ft (10,730 m); range 821 km (510 miles) with standard fuel

WEIGHTS: empty 9800 lb (4445 kg); normal take-off 11,400 lb (5171 kg)

DIMENSIONS: span 41 ft 7 in (12.67 m); length 31 ft 11 in (9.73 m); height 15 ft 4 in (4.67 m)

ARMAMENT: twelve .303 in (7.7 mm) fixed forward-firing machine guns with 500 rounds per gun in the wing

The Hawker Typhoon exuded power, as seen in this photograph in which the aircraft's four .787 in (20 mm) cannons are visible.

The Typhoon was possibly the Western Allies' finest ground-attack fighter of World War II. In another light it may be regarded as a distinct failure, as it had been planned as a heavily armed interceptor to succeed the Hawker Hurricane and Supermarine Spitfire. A cantilever low-wing monoplane of basically all-metal stressed-skin construction with retractable tailwheel landing gear, the Typhoon was finally planned in two forms with the Napier Sabre liquid-cooled H-type engine and the Bristol Centaurus air-cooled radial engine, the latter becoming the Tempest. First flown in prototype form in February 1940, the Typhoon did not fly in Mk IA production form

(105 aircraft) until May 1941 and entered service in June of the same year, initially proving a failure as a result of a structural weakness in the tail and wholly indifferent performance at altitude as a result of its thick wing.

Definitive version

The Typhoon Mk IB was the definitive version of the Typhoon. The fixed forward-firing armament was revised to four .787 in (20 mm) cannons with 140 rounds per gun in the wing, the original type of framed canopy with a side door was replaced (from 1943) by a clear-view bubble canopy with a rearward-sliding access section, and the engine replaced by the uprated Sabre II, generally driving a four- rather than three-blade propeller.

This Typhoon Mk 1b is seen in the markings of No. 181 Squadron, which used the aircraft in the bombing role after the D-Day invasion.

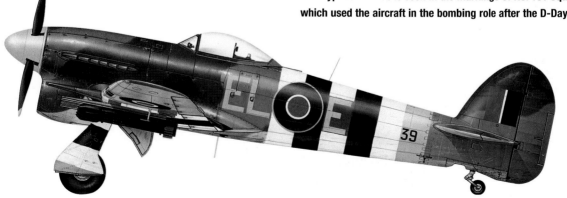

Lavochkin LaGG-1 and LaGG-3

It was not until 1939–40 that the prototypes of Soviet fighters that could really be classed as modern made their appearance. The first was the LaGG-1 (I-22), which took its name from the initials of the three engineers who conceived it: Lavochkin, Gorbunov and Gudkov.

COUNTRY OF ORIGIN: USSR

TYPE: (LaGG-3) single-seat fighter and fighter-bomber

POWERPLANT: one 1260 hp (939.5 kW) Klimov VK-105PF-1 12-cylinder Vee engine

PERFORMANCE: maximum speed 357 mph (575 km/h); climb to 16,405 ft (5000 m) in 5 minutes 48 seconds; service ceiling 31,825 ft (9700 m); range 621 miles (1000 km)

WEIGHTS: empty 5776 lb (2620 kg); maximum take-off 7032 lb (3190 kg)

DIMENSIONS: span 32 ft 1.75 in (9.80 m); length 28 ft 11 in (8.81 m); height 8 ft 4 in (2.54 m)

ARMAMENT: one .787 in (20 mm) fixed forward-firing cannon in an engine installation and two .3 in (7.62 mm) fixed forward-firing machine guns in the upper part of the forward fuselage, plus an external bomb and rocket load of 441 lb (200 kg)

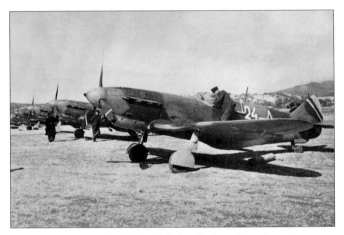

LaGG-3s of the 9th IAP (Fighter Aviation Regiment) serving on the Black Sea front. The LaGG did not fare well in combat.

The LaGG-1 was one of several new monoplane fighters whose development was ordered by the Soviet authorities in 1939 in an effort to modernize the Soviet air forces at a time of deepening European crisis.

Rushed into production
Based on a wooden airframe, the LaGG-1 was a "modern" monoplane fighter in its low-wing layout with an enclosed cockpit and retractable main landing-gear units. The prototype first flew in March 1940, and trials revealed good speed but poor acceleration, climb rate, range,

service ceiling and handling. Even so, the type was rushed into production; no fewer than 100 interim LaGG-1 and 6427 slightly improved LaGG-3 fighters being completed by the autumn of 1941. The LaGG-1 still equipped two air regiments at the time of the German invasion of June 1941, but it was the LaGG-3 that held the line during the first critical months of the German onslaught. The LaGG-3 was active in the air defense of Leningrad.

This LaGG-3 is wearing the camouflage scheme that was typical of Soviet fighters in the summer of 1941.

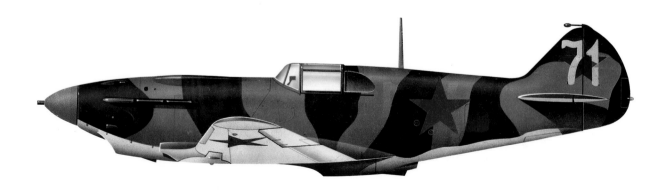

Yakovlev Yak-1

Yak-1 Krasavyets (Beauty) made its first public appearance during an air display on November 7, 1940. It was Aleksandr S. Yakovlev's first fighter design, and it earned him the Order of Lenin, the gift of a Zis car and a prize of 100,000 roubles.

The Yak-1 was light and responsive on the controls, but the pilot's view from the cockpit was seriously restricted.

COUNTRY OF ORIGIN: USSR

TYPE: (Yak-1 early production standard) single-seat fighter and fighter-bomber

POWERPLANT: one 1100 hp (820 kW) Klimov M-105P 12-cylinder Vee engine

PERFORMANCE: maximum speed 373 mph (600 km/h); climb to 16,405 ft (5000 m) in 5 minutes 24 seconds; service ceiling 32,810 ft (10,000 m); range 435 miles (700 km)

WEIGHTS: empty 5174 lb (2347 kg); maximum take-off 6276 lb (2847 kg)

DIMENSIONS: span 32 ft 9.7 in (10 m); length 27 ft 9.9 in (8.48 m); height 8 ft 8 in (2.64 m)

ARMAMENT: one .787 in (20 mm) fixed forward-firing cannon in an engine installation, and two .3 in (7.62 mm) fixed forward-firing machine guns in the upper part of the forward fuselage, plus an external bomb and rocket load of 441 lb (200 kg)

First flown during January 1940, the Yak-1 lightweight fighter was one of the most important and successful fighters fielded by the USSR in the course of World War II. Like many of its Soviet contemporaries, it was based on an airframe of mixed light alloy and wooden construction.

Finest Soviet fighters

The Yak-1 had a typical "modern" fighter design, with a cantilever low-set wing, enclosed cockpit and retractable main landing-gear units. It entered production late in 1940 and 8721 aircraft were delivered by the summer of 1943. The main models were the baseline Yak-1, the Yak-1B with a cut-down rear fuselage allowing the incorporation of a clear-view bubble canopy, and the Yak-1M lightened model with a number of significant improvements.

Developments were the Yak-3, Yak-7 and Yak-9. This series of fighters was the finest available to the Soviet air forces during the eastern campaign, and undoubtedly helped to turn the tide of the war. As well as being an interceptor, the Yak-3 was used in close support of ground forces, and for the escort of Pe-2 and Il-2 assault aircraft, one formation of Yak-3s preceding the bombers and attacking German fighter airfields while another gave closer escort. The Yak-3 airframe was later fitted with a turbojet engine to become the Yak-15, Russia's first operational jet fighter.

The inscription on this 37th IAP Yak-1B reads: "To the pilot of the Stalingrad Front Guards Major Comrade B.M. Yeremin, from the collective farm workers 'Stakhanov,' Comrade Golovatov."

Mikoyan MiG-1 and MiG-3

The MiG-1 was developed to meet a Soviet Air Force requirement, issued in 1938, for a high-altitude fighter, and although it was unstable and difficult to fly it was rushed into production because of its high performance.

COUNTRY OF ORIGIN: USSR

TYPE: (MiG-3) single-seat fighter and fighter-bomber

POWERPLANT: one 1350 hp (1007 kW) Mikulin AM-35A 12-cylinder Vee engine

PERFORMANCE: maximum speed 398 mph (640 km/h); climb to 16,405 ft (5000 m) in 5 minutes 42 seconds; service ceiling 39,370 ft (12,000 m); range 742 miles (1195 km)

WEIGHTS: empty 5721 lb (2595 kg); maximum take-off 7385 lb (3350 kg)

DIMENSIONS: span 33 ft 5.5 in (10.2 m); length 27 ft .8 in (8.25 m); height 8 ft 8.33 in (2.65 m)

ARMAMENT: one .5 in (12.7 mm) and two .3 in (7.62 mm) fixed forward-firing machine guns in the upper part of the forward fuselage, plus an external bomb and rocket load of 441 lb (200 kg)

The MiG-3 had a good performance at low level, which made it ideal for the tactical reconnaissance role.

The MiG-1 and MiG-3 series of aircraft were placed in large-scale production because, even though they were extremely difficult to fly, they possessed very high performance.

High-altitude fighter

The MiG-1 was developed for an urgent Soviet air force requirement, issued early in 1938, for a high-altitude fighter, and first flew in prototype form in April 1940. Production totalled 100 aircraft, with the armament of one .5 in (12.7 mm) and two .3 in (7.62 mm) machine guns and either open or enclosed accommodation. These were followed by the improved MiG-3 of which 3322 were delivered up to

spring 1942 with improved protective features, a rearward-sliding rather than side-hinged canopy, and increased dihedral. Because of the increased combat radius that resulted from the provision of an auxiliary fuel tank, MiG-3s were used extensively for fighter reconnaissance. The next MiG fighter design, the MiG-5, was basically a MiG-3 with a Shvetsov M-82A radial engine and was produced only in small numbers in 1943, the La-5 being selected for mass production in preference.

Camouflaged for winter operations, this MiG-3 bears the legend "Za Rodinu" (For the Homeland) on the side of its fuselage.

Kawasaki Ki-61 Hien "Tony"

The Kawasaki Ki.61 was designed to replace the Nakajima Ki.43 Hayabusa (Oscar) in Japanese army service. Named Hien (Swallow), it was the only operational Japanese fighter to feature an inverted-Vee engine.

COUNTRY OF ORIGIN: Japan

TYPE: (Ki-61-Ib) single-seat fighter

POWERPLANT: one 1175 hp (876 kW) Kawasaki Ha-40 (Army Type 2) 12-cylinder inverted-Vee engine

PERFORMANCE: maximum speed 368 mph (592 km/h); climb to 16,405 ft (5000 m) in 5 minutes 31 seconds; service ceiling 37,730 ft (11,600 m); range 684 miles (1100 km)

WEIGHTS: empty 4872 lb (2210 kg); normal take-off 6504 lb (2950 kg); maximum take-off 7165 lb (3250 kg)

DIMENSIONS: Span 39 ft 4.25 in (12 m); length 28 ft 8.5 in (8.75 m); height 12 ft 1.75 in (3.70 m)

ARMAMENT: two .5 in (12.7 mm) fixed forward-firing machine guns in the upper part of the forward fuselage and two .5 in (12.7 mm) fixed forward-firing machine guns in the leading edges of the wing

The prototype Hien flew in December 1941 and the aircraft went into full production some six months later.

The Hien was encountered mainly in Burma, the Philippines and in the defense of the Japanese homeland in 1945. The Hien was unique among Japanese first-line warplanes of World War II in being powered by an inverted-Vee piston engine. This was a Kawasaki Ha-40 unit, a license-built version of the German Daimler-Benz DB 601A. The Allied code name assigned by the United States war department was "Tony."

Excellent performance and good handling

The first of 12 prototype and pre-production aircraft flew in December 1941, and revealed excellent performance and good handling. The Ki-61-I entered service in February 1943, and 1380 aircraft were delivered in two subvariants with different armament, before the advent of 1274 Ki-61 Kai fighters. Further development resulted in the Ki-61-II Kai optimized for high-altitude operations with the Kawasaki Ha-140 engine, 374 aircraft in two subvariants were delivered. Like other Japanese fighters, it was soon eclipsed by its American counterparts. This became the Ki-100, which was without doubt the Imperial Japanese Army Air Force's finest fighter.

Seen here is Ki-61 of the HQ Chutai, 244th Sentai, Chofu, Tokyo, assigned to air defense duties.

Republic P-47 Thunderbolt

The Republic Thunderbolt, a truly great fighter of World War II, was designed around the most powerful engine then available, the new 2000 hp (1491 kW) Pratt & Whitney Double Wasp radial.

COUNTRY OF ORIGIN: USA

TYPE: (P-47M) single-seat interceptor fighter

POWERPLANT: one 2100 hp (1566 kW) Pratt & Whitney R-2800-57(C) 18-cylinder two-row radial engine

PERFORMANCE: maximum speed 470 mph (756 km/h); initial climb rate 3500 ft (1067 m) per minute; service ceiling not available; range 560 miles (901 km)

WEIGHTS: empty 10,423 lb (4728 kg); maximum take-off 15,500 lb (7031 kg)

DIMENSIONS: span 40 ft 9 in (12.42 m); length 36 ft 1 in (10.99 m); height 14 ft 7 in (4.44 m)

ARMAMENT: six or eight .5 in (12.7 mm) fixed forward-firing machine guns in the leading edges of the wing

This P-47 was donated by public subscription, as the inscription on its fuselage indicates.

The Thunderbolt, a classic World War II warplane, is an enduring example of the American predilection to "think big" and produce an item that is visually impressive yet packed with equally impressive capability.

Uprated powerplant and bubble canopy

The XP-47B prototype first flew in May 1941, but despite indications of impressive performance a number of serious design problems had to be resolved before the P-47B could enter combat service in April 1943. The 171 P-47B

This uncamouflaged P-47 served in the Italian theater of operations, where colorful tail markings were common.

fighters and 602 generally similar P-47C fighter-bombers were powered by the 2000 hp (1491 kW) R-2800-21 engine, while the definitive P-47D introduced an uprated powerplant and, in its major subvariant, a clear-view bubble canopy in place of the original framed canopy and razorback rear fuselage. Production of the P-47D and generally similar P-47G razorback model totalled 12,603 and 354 respectively. When the Germans started firing the Fieseler Fi 103 (or V-1) flying bomb at the southern part of the UK in June 1944, the USAAF decided to procure a sprint version of the P-47D as the P-47M (130 built) with the R-2800-57(C) radial engine offering an emergency combat rating of 2800 hp (2088 kW). The last version of the Thunderbolt to be built was the P-47N, largest and heaviest of all Thunderbolt variants. In addition to service with the USAAF during the war the Thunderbolt was used by Brazil, the Free French Air Force, the British Royal Air Force and the Soviet Union.

Messerschmitt Me 262

Design work on the Me 262, the world's first operational jet fighter, began in September 1939. Six years were to elapse between the 262 taking shape on Messerschmitt's drawing board and its entry into Luftwaffe service.

COUNTRY OF ORIGIN: Germany

TYPE: (262A-1A) single-seat air-superiority fighter

POWERPLANT: two 1984 lb (900 kg) Junkers Jumo 004B-1, –2 or –3 turbojets

PERFORMANCE: maximum speed at 19,685 ft (6000 m) 540 mph (869 km/h); service ceiling above 40,000 ft (12,190 m); range 652 miles (1050 km)

WEIGHTS: empty 8,378 lb (3795 kg); maximum take-off 14,080 lb (6387 kg)

DIMENSIONS: span 40 ft 11.5 in (12.5 m); length 34 ft 9.5 in (10.58 m); height 12 ft 7 in (3.83 m); wing area 234 sq ft (21.73 sq m)

ARMAMENT: four 1.18 in (30 mm) Rheinmetall-Borsig Mk 108A-3 cannons with 100 rounds for upper pair and 80 rounds for the lower; provision for 12 R4M air-to-air rockets under each wing

Aerodynamically, the Me 262 was a beautiful aircraft, as is evident in this photograph.

The Me 262 was undoubtedly the most advanced jet aircraft to see combat service during World War II, and certainly the most successful in combat. Messerschmitt were somewhat late in getting off the mark in designing a jet combat aircraft. Heinkel were well advanced with the development of the He 280 prototype when in January 1939 Messerschmitt were ordered by the RLM to begin development of a similar type of aircraft. The turbojet engines then available lacked sufficient power to be used singly, and so the design mounted twin-turbojets in underwing nacelles. The Me 262 V7 was the immediate precursor to a production model, the Me 262A-1a. This aircraft was the standard interceptor version, and first flew in combat on October 3, 1944.

The end of the war in sight

By the autumn of 1943, the outcome of the war was decided, but the decision was taken to convert many Me 262-A1a's in service to the later A-2a standard, by fitting Schloss 503A-1 bomb racks under the wings.

This is a Me 262A-1a of JG 7, which became fully operational with the jet fighter early in 1945.

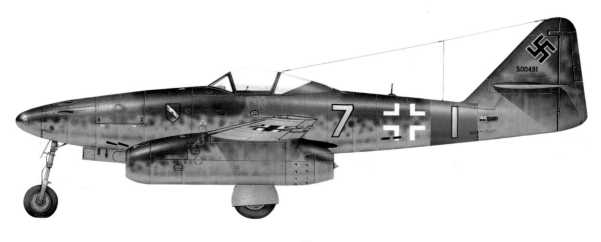

Messerschmitt Me 163 Komet

The Me 163 Komet was based on the experimental DFS 194, designed in 1938 by Professor Alexander Lippisch and transferred, together with its design staff, to the Messerschmitt company for further development.

COUNTRY OF ORIGIN: Germany

TYPE: single-seat interceptor

POWERPLANT: one 3750 lb (1700 kg) Walter HWK 509A-2 bi-propellant rocket burning concentrated hydrogen peroxide and hydrazine/methanol

PERFORMANCE: maximum speed at 32,800 ft (10,000 m) 596 mph (960 km/h); service ceiling 54,000 ft (16,500 m); range under 62 miles (100 km); endurance about eight minutes in total

WEIGHTS: empty 4191 lb (1905 kg); maximum loaded 9042 lb (4110 kg)

DIMENSIONS: span 30 ft 7 in (9.3 m); length 18 ft 8 in (5.69 m); height 9 ft (2.74 m)

ARMAMENT: two 11.81 in (300 mm) MK 108 cannons with 60 rounds each

This photograph shows an Me 163 being recovered after touching down on its landing skid.

Known as the "Kraft Ei" (Power Egg) by its pilots, the Me 163 had very good flight characteristics. Landing was the problem, as any residual fuel could cause an explosion.

The Me 163 was radical and futuristic. The concept of the short-endurance high-speed interceptor powered by a rocket engine was certainly valid and could have been more of an adversary than it was.

Violent explosions on landing

The first flight of Dr. Alex Lippisch's radical fighter, bereft of a horizontal tail and with an incredibly short fuselage, was made in glider form in the spring of 1941. To propel the aircraft, two extremely volatile liquids were employed, which ignited when they came into contact. To save weight the Komet took off from a wheeled trolley and landed on a sprung skid. The landing impact often caused any residual propellants to slosh together causing a violent explosion. The first rocket-powered flight was made in August 1941, and during subsequent trials the Me 163 broke all existing world air-speed records, reaching speeds of up to 620 mph (1000 km/h). In May 1944 an operational Komet unit, JG400, began forming at Wittmundhaven and Venlo. Many Me 163s were lost in landing accidents. About 300 Komets were built, but JG400 remained the only operational unit and the rocket fighter recorded only nine kills during its brief career. A principal problem was the aircraft's high closing speed, which made an accurate interception extremely difficult.

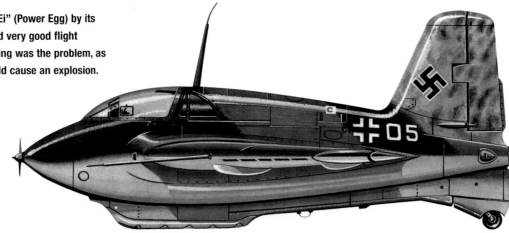

Grumman F6F Hellcat

The Grumman Hellcat has an assured place in history as the fighter that changed the course of the Pacific air war. Before the Hellcat made its operational debut, it was the Mitsubishi Zero that had ruled the Pacific sky.

The most successful fighter of the Pacific campaign, shooting down 5156 Japanese aircraft for the loss of only 270 of its own number in air-to-air combat, the F6F was designed from the spring of 1941 as an F4F successor. The F6F was an enlarged and better streamlined F4F with a considerably more potent engine, and the XF6F-3 first prototype flew in June 1942. The F6F-3 initial production model (4402 aircraft including 205 F6F-3N night-fighters and 18 radar-equipped F6F-3E night intruders) entered combat in August 1943, and revealed high performance, hard-hitting firepower, great strength and adequate agility.

The Grumman Hellcat was initially rejected by the US Navy, but went on to become one of the toughest combat aircraft ever built.

COUNTRY OF ORIGIN: USA

TYPE: (F6F-3): single-seat carrierborne fighter and fighter-bomber

POWERPLANT: one 2000 hp (1491 kW) Pratt & Whitney R-2800-10 or -10W Double Wasp 18-cylinder two-row radial engine

PERFORMANCE: maximum speed 375 mph (603 km/h); initial climb rate 3500 ft (1067 m) per minute; service ceiling 38,400 ft (11705 m); range 1590 miles (2559 km)

WEIGHTS: empty 4128kg (9101lb); maximum take-off 7025kg (15,487lb)

DIMENSIONS: span 42 ft 10 in (13.06 m); length 33 ft 7 in (10.24 m); height 13 ft 1 in (3.99 m)

ARMAMENT: six .5 in (12.7 mm) fixed forward-firing machine guns in the leading edges of the wing, plus an external bomb load of 1000 lb (454 kg)

Prominent in US Navy operations

Some 252 of the standard fighters were transferred under Lend-Lease to the UK for service with the Fleet Air Arm with the designation Gannet Mk I soon changed to Hellcat Mk I. In the Pacific, the Hellcat played a prominent role in all US naval operations, in particular the Battle of the Philippine Sea (June 19–20, 1944). In this action, naval aircraft from nine Japanese aircraft carriers, together with shore-based aircraft, launched a massive air attack against the US Task Force 58. In a battle that became known as the "Marianas Turkey Shoot," American combat air patrols and AA fire destroyed 325 enemy aircraft, including 220 of the 328 launched by the carriers.

The addition of an auxiliary fuel tank gave the Hellcat the "long legs" it needed for operations over the Pacific.

Lavochkin La-5

The Lavochkin La-5 was developed from the earlier LaGG-3 in response to a desperate requirement for the Soviet Air Force for a modern fighter that could hold its own with the Messerschmitt 109.

COUNTRY OF ORIGIN: USSR

TYPE: (La-5FN) single-seat fighter and fighter-bomber

POWERPLANT: one 1630 hp (1215 kW) Shvetsov ASh-82FN 14-cylinder two-row radial engine

PERFORMANCE: maximum speed 403 mph (648 km/h); climb to 16,405 ft (5000 m) in 5 minutes; service ceiling 36,090 ft (11,000 m); range 475 miles (765 km)

WEIGHTS: empty 5743 lb (2605 kg); normal take-off 7198 lb (3265 kg); maximum take-off 7500 lb (3402 kg)

DIMENSIONS: span 32 ft 1.75 in (9.80 m); length 28 ft 5.33 in (8.67 m); height 8 ft 4 in (2.54 m)

ARMAMENT: two .787 in (20 mm) fixed forward-firing cannons in the upper part of the forward fuselage, plus an external bomb and rocket load of 1102 lb (500 kg)

The Lavochkin La-5 gave the Soviet Air Force the edge over the Luftwaffe from 1943 onward.

The LaGG-3 mentioned previously was an indifferent fighter of wooden construction that was easy to build and provided adequate capability. The La-5 was a superb fighter, however, which offered truly excellent capabilities through the replacement of the LaGG-3's Klimov M-105 Vee engine by the Shvetsov M-82 radial engine.

Better all-around performer

The change was ordered in August 1941, and the first of several prototypes flew in March 1942. Intensive development led to an early start to the production run, which lasted until late 1994 and amounted to 9920 aircraft

This green-brown camouflage scheme was standard on most La-5s except in winter, when white was applied.

in variants, such as the La-5 with the 1480 hp (1103.5 kW) M-82A engine, the La-5F with the 1540 hp (1148 kW) M-82F (later ASh-82F) engine, the definitive La-5FN, the La-5FN Type 41 with a metal rather than wooden wing, and the La-5UTI two-seat conversion trainer, of which only a few were completed. Early combats showed that the La-5 was a better all-around performer than the Messerschmitt 109G. Lavochkin undertook some redesign work to reduce the fighter's weight, and re-engined it with the 1510 hp (1126 kW) M-82FN direct-injection engine, which endowed the La-5 with better climbing characteristics and maneuverability. The modified aircraft, designated La-5FN, made its appearance at the front in March 1943, and soon began to make its presence felt in the hands of some very competent Soviet fighter pilots. Among them was Ivan Kozhedub, who made his combat debut just before the battle of Kursk in the summer of 1943 and who went on to score 62 kills while flying Lavochkin fighters, making him the top-scoring Allied air ace.

Heinkel He 219 Uhu

In the first half of 1943, General Josef Kammhuber pressed for the production of new twin-engined types designed specifically for night-fighting. At the forefront of these was the Heinkel He 219 Uhu (Owl).

COUNTRY OF ORIGIN: Germany

TYPE: (He 219A-7/R1) two-seat night-fighter

POWERPLANT: two 1900 hp (1417 kW) Daimler-Benz DB 603G 12-cylinder inverted-Vee engines

PERFORMANCE: maximum speed 416 mph (670 km/h); initial climb rate 1810 ft (552 m) per minute; service ceiling 41,665 ft (12,700 m); range 1243 miles (2000 km)

WEIGHTS: empty 24,692 lb (11,200 kg); maximum take-off 33,730 lb (15,300 kg)

DIMENSIONS: span 60 ft 8.33 in (18.5 m); length 50 ft 11.75 in (15.54 m); height 13 ft 5.5 in (4.1 m)

ARMAMENT: two 1.18 in (30 mm) fixed forward-firing cannons in the wing roots, two 1.18 in (30 mm) and two .787 in (20 mm) fixed forward-firing cannons in a ventral tray, and two 1.18 in (30 mm) obliquely upward/forward-firing in the upper part of the rear fuselage

This photograph clearly shows the arrangement of the He 219's nose-mounted "Lichtenstein" radar aerial array.

The Uhu (Owl) was the finest German night-fighter of World War II, but was built only in very small numbers as a result of political antipathy to the Heinkel company, which continued to develop and build the type despite orders not to do so. Design of the He 219 began in 1940 as a multi-role warplane, and it was only late in 1941 that the type became a dedicated night-fighter.

First aircraft equipped with ejection seats
The first of 10 prototypes flew in November 1942, and by this time there were orders for 300 He 219A initial production aircraft including an initial 130 He 219A-0

pre-production machines. The first production model was the He 219A-2, and over 150 He 219A aircraft were built in variants up to the He 219A-7 for limited service from the middle of 1943. On June 11, 1943, Major Werner Streib shot down five Avro Lancasters in a single sortie, and in the first six sorties flown by his unit 20 aircraft were shot down. Armed with six .787 in (20 mm) cannon and equipped with the latest AI radar, the He 219 would certainly have torn great gaps in the ranks of the RAF's night bombers had it been available in quantity. It also had a performance comparable to that of the Mosquito, which other German night-fighters did not, and could therefore have fought the RAF's night intruders on equal terms. The He 219 was the first operational aircraft to be equipped with ejection seats, and a German crew is thought to have used these on one occasion after being shot down by a Mosquito.

Seen here is a Heinkel He 219 of Nachtjagdgeschwader 1, based at Venlo on the Dutch-German border.

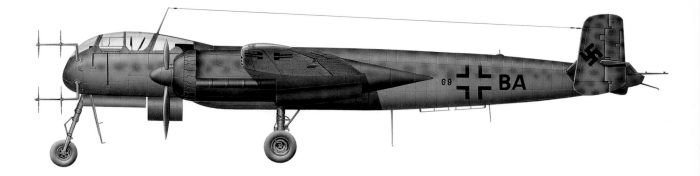

Hawker Tempest

First flown in 1943, the Hawker Tempest V was the fastest, most powerful fighter in the world when it entered RAF service in April 1944. In June that year, Tempest squadrons were assigned to defend against V-1 flying bombs.

An extremely powerful fighter, the Hawker Tempest V was designed for medium- and low-level air superiority operations.

COUNTRY OF ORIGIN: United Kingdom

TYPE: (Tempest Mk V) single-seat fighter and fighter-bomber

POWERPLANT: one 2260 hp (1685 kW) Napier Sabre IIA, IIB or IIC 24-cylinder H-type engine

PERFORMANCE: maximum speed 435 mph (700 km/h); climb to 20,000 ft (6095 m) in 6 minutes 6 seconds; service ceiling 36,000 ft (10,975 m); range 1300 miles (2092 km)

WEIGHTS: empty 10,700 lb (4854 kg); normal take-off 11,510 lb (5221 kg); maximum take-off 13,640 lb (6187 kg)

DIMENSIONS: span 41 ft (12.50 m); length 33 ft 8 in (10.26 m); height 16 ft 1 in (4.9 m)

ARMAMENT: four .787 in (20 mm) fixed forward-firing cannons in the leading edges of the wing, plus an external bomb and rocket load of 2000 lb (907 kg)

The Tempest was the third Hawker fighter to enjoy operational status in World War II. Not as well known as the preceding Hurricane and Typhoon, it was an excellent warplane that proved highly adaptable in terms of its production in variants with air-cooled and liquid-cooled engines. Planned as an advanced fighter to undertake the interceptor role in which the Typhoon had failed, the Tempest was a generally similar airplane except for its significantly thinner wing and longer fuselage.

Post-war target tugs
It first flew in prototype form during September 1942, retaining the chin radiator of the Typhoon. The type entered service as the Tempest Mk V in April 1944. The Tempest Mk V Series 1 (100 aircraft) had protruding cannon muzzles, but the Tempest Mk V Series 2 (700 aircraft) had cannon muzzles flush with the wing's leading edges. After the war some were converted for use as target tugs and designated Tempest TT.Mk 5. As the Tempest Mk V was entering production, Hawker was pressing ahead with new improved models, especially the Tempest Mk II with a Centaurus radial engine. Powerplant development proved difficult, and the first of an eventual 472 Tempest Mk II aircraft was completed only in October 1944 after production had been switched from Gloucester to Bristol.

This is a Tempest Mk V of No. 3 Squadron wearing post-war markings. The squadron was based in Germany for most of its career after 1944.

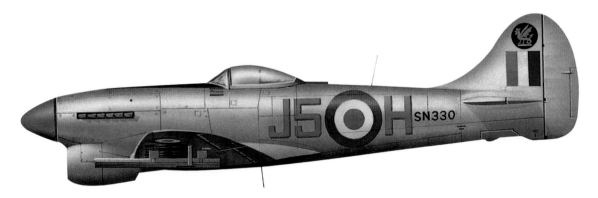

Kawanishi N1K1 Shiden "George"

Known by the Allied code name George, the Shiden was a land-based fighter developed from the Kyofu fighter floatplane. The Shiden proved to be one of the finest fighter aircraft to see action in the Pacific theater.

Had it been available in sufficient numbers at an earlier date, the Shiden could have made a real impact on the Pacific air war.

COUNTRY OF ORIGIN: Japan

TYPE: (N1K1-J) single-seat fighter and fighter-bomber

POWERPLANT: one 1990 hp (1557 kW) Nakajima NK9H Homare 21 18-cylinder two-row radial engine

PERFORMANCE: maximum speed 361 mph (581 km/h); climb to 19,685 ft (6000 m) in 7 minutes 50 seconds; service ceiling 41,010 ft (12,500 m); range 1581 miles (2544 km)

WEIGHTS: empty 6387 lb (2897 kg); maximum take-off 9526 lb (4321 kg)

DIMENSIONS: span 39 ft 4.5 in (12 m); length 29 ft 1.88 in (8.88 m); height 13 ft 3.85 in (4.06 m)

ARMAMENT: two .787 in (20 mm) fixed forward-firing cannons in the leading edges of the wing, two .787 in (20 mm) fixed forward-firing cannon in underwing gondolas, and two .303 in (7.7 mm) fixed forward-firing machine guns in the forward fuselage, plus an external bomb load of 265 lb (120 kg)

The Shiden (Violet Lightning) resulted when Kawanishi's design team realized in December 1941 that its N1K1 Kyofu floatplane fighter, which had yet to fly, had so much potential a landplane derivative was clearly a possibility.

Temperamental engine

There followed nine prototypes. The first flew in December 1942, before the delivery of 1098 N1K1-J production aircraft in three subvariants. These entered service early in 1944, and were later complemented by 415 examples of the two subvariants of the N1K2-J with a redesigned fuselage

and tail unit as well as the wing position lowered to allow the use of shorter main landing-gear units. The N1K proved an effective fighter but it was troubled by a temperamental engine. Both operational models were prominent in the Philippines, around Formosa and in the defense of the Japanese home islands. Production totaled 1098 N1K1-Js and 415 N1K2-Js. In the hands of a skilled pilot the Shiden was a formidable weapon; in February 1945, for example, the Japanese ace Kaneyoshi Muto engaged 12 US Navy Hellcats single-handed and destroyed four of them, forcing the others to break off combat.

Seen here is a late-production N1K2-J Kai of the 343rd Kokutai, Imperial Japanese Navy Air force during 1945.

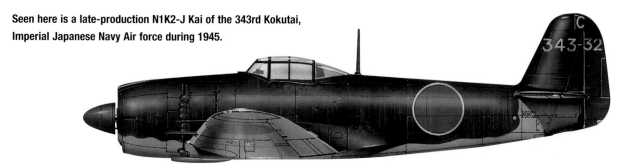

de Havilland Vampire

Design work on the DH.100 Vampire began in May 1942, the prototype flying on September 20, 1943. It became the first Allied jet aircraft capable of sustained speeds over 500 mph (804 km/h) over a wide altitude range.

COUNTRY OF ORIGIN: United Kingdom/Switzerland

TYPE: (FB MK6) single-seat fighter-bomber

POWERPLANT: one 3300 lb (1498 kg) de Havilland Goblin 35 turbojet

PERFORMANCE: maximum speed 548 mph (883 km/h); service ceiling 44,000 ft (13,410 m); range with drop tanks 1400 miles (2253 km)

WEIGHTS: empty 7200 lb (3266 kg); loaded with drop tanks 12,290 lb (5600 kg)

DIMENSIONS: span 38 ft (11.6 m); length 30 ft 9 in (9.37 m); height 8 ft 10 in (2.69 m); wing area 262 sq ft (24.32 sq m)

ARMAMENT: four .787 in (20 mm) Hispano cannons with 150 rounds, wing pylons capable of carrying either two 500 lb (227 kg) bombs or 60 lb (27.2 kg) rocket projectiles

Drop-tank trials on the Vampire led to the standardization of the 100-gallon, pylon-mounted cylindrical type.

The first production Vampire flew in April 1945. After the first 50 aircraft the F.1 was fitted with a pressurized cockpit and a bubble canopy in place of the earlier three-piece hood. The Vampire Mk 2 was a Mk 1 airframe fitted with a Rolls-Royce Nene turbojet and did not enter service, only three being built. It was followed by the Vampire F.3, a long-range version with extra internal fuel, underwing tanks and a de Havilland Goblin 2 turbojet; 85 were supplied to the RCAF, four to Norway and 12 to Mexico, and the type was built under license in India. The Nene-engined F.Mk.4 was to have been the production version of the Mk 2 and was developed into the F.30/31 built under license for the RAAF. The first F.30 was delivered to

the RAAF on September 26, 1949; 57 were built, followed by 23 FB.31 fighter-bombers, and more than half the F.30s were later modified to FB.31 standard.

Ground-attack variant

The first Vampire variant developed for ground attack was the FB.5. As the FB.6, fitted with a Goblin 3 engine, it was widely exported. The Vampire FB.5 remained in RAF service until 1957. The Vampire FB.9 was a tropicalized version of the FB.5 and was used by the RAF, RNZAF, SAAF, RRAF and India. The Vampire NF.10 was a night-fighter, serving with the RAF and the Italian Air Force, in whose service it was designated Mk.54. The Sea Vampire F.20 and F.21 were navalized versions. The T.11 was a two-seat trainer. One of the biggest overseas Vampire users was France, which built the Nene-engined Vampire Mk 53 as the Mistral.

This is the prototype Vampire, LG548/G. The "G" meant that the aircraft had to be kept under constant armed guard.

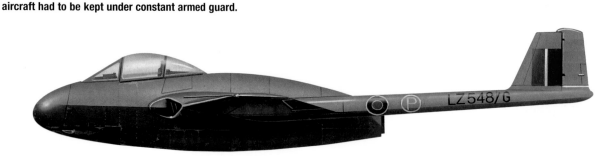

Gloster Meteor

The Gloster Meteor, the RAF's first operational jet fighter, traced its lineage to the first British experimental jet, the Gloster E.28/39, which first flew on May 15, 1941, under the power of a single Whittle W.2/7000 turbojet.

One of the Meteor's attributes was its excellent rate of climb.

The Meteor was Gloster's answer to Air Ministry specification F.9/40, calling for a single-seat interceptor powered by gas turbine engines. The low thrust output of the engines available at the time dictated a twin-engine configuration, but apart from the radical nature of its form of propulsion the Meteor was entirely conventional in design. Twelve prototypes were ordered and eight were completed, the first flying in March 1943.

New world air-speed record

The aircraft was powered by two 1500 lb (680 kg) thrust Halford H.1 turbojets, but the first 20 production aircraft were fitted with the 1700 lb (771 kg) Rolls-Royce Welland. Twelve of these were issued to No. 616 Squadron, which deployed to Manston and flew its first "Diver" (anti V-1) patrol on 27 July. The Meteor destroyed only 13 V-1s, but it came very late to the battle and it was underpowered. The next variant, the Meteor F.3, was a much better proposition, using the 2000 lb (906 kg) thrust Rolls-Royce Derwent I engine; but deliveries to No. 616 Squadron did not begin until December 1944. The Mk 3 version was followed into service by the Meteor F.Mk.4.

COUNTRY OF ORIGIN: United Kingdom

TYPE: single-seat fighter

POWERPLANT: two 3,600 lb (1,587 kg) Rolls Royce Derwent 8 turbojets

PERFORMANCE: maximum speed at 33,000 ft (10,000 m) 598 mph (962 km/h); service ceiling 43,000 ft (13,106 m); range 980 miles (1580 km)

WEIGHTS: empty 10,626 lb (4820 kg); loaded 19,100 lb (8664 kg)

DIMENSIONS: span 37 ft 2 in (11.32 m); length 44 ft 7 in (13.58 m); height 13 ft (3.96 m)

ARMAMENT: four .787 in (20 mm) Hispano cannons, foreign F.8s were often modified to carry two iron bombs, eight rockets, or other offensive stores

Powered by two Rolls-Royce Derwent 5s, the F.Mk.4 first flew in April 1945. In November, it set up a new world air-speed record of 606 mph (975 km/h). It was the first Meteor mark to be exported, being supplied to Argentina, Holland, Belgium and Denmark. The most prolific of the Meteor variants was the F.Mk.8. This version was also the subject of major export orders, going to Egypt, Belgium, Denmark, Syria, Holland, Brazil and Israel. The F.8 also equipped No. 77 Squadron RAAF. The Meteor FR.9 was a fighter-reconnaissance variant, while the PR.10 was an unarmed photo-reconnaissance aircraft. The Meteors NF.11, NF.12, NF.13 and NF.14 were night-fighters, with AI radar; the U.15-U.21 were target drones; the TT.20 was a target tug; and the T.7 was a two-seat trainer. Meteor production, all variants, totalled 3545 aircraft.

The Gloster F9/40, seen here, was the prototype of the fighter that became the Meteor.

Saab J21A and J21R

Although Sweden had been mostly reliant on foreign combat types before and during World War II, the Swedish aircraft manufacturer, SAAB, had produced an indigenous fighter aircraft, the J21A.

COUNTRY OF ORIGIN: Sweden

TYPE: (J21A-1) single-seat interceptor fighter

POWERPLANT: one 1100 kW (1475 hp) SFA DB 605B 12-cylinder Vee engine

PERFORMANCE: maximum speed 401 mph (645 km/h); initial climb rate 2789 ft (850 m) per minute; service ceiling 36,090 ft (11,000 m); range 466 miles (750 km)

WEIGHTS: empty 7165 lb (3250 kg); maximum take-off 9730 lb (4413 kg)

DIMENSIONS: span 38 ft 0.75 in (11.60 m); length 34 ft 3.25 in (10.44 m); height 13 ft 3.25 in (3.97 m)

ARMAMENT: one .787 in (20 mm) fixed forward-firing cannon and two .52 in (13.2 mm) fixed forward-firing machine guns in the nose, and two .52 in (13.2 mm) fixed forward-firing machine guns in the front of the booms

The Saab J21A/R had only a brief career as a fighter aircraft, being replaced by the J29.

Sweden wished to ensure its continued neutrality through a policy of armed strength during World War II but was effectively denied access to foreign weapons. In response Sweden undertook an indigenous rearmament program including an advanced fighter, and for this task the Saab 21 was ultimately produced.

Low-wing monoplane
It was designed round a license-produced version of the Daimler-Benz DB 605B engine as a low-wing monoplane with tricycle landing gear, heavy forward-firing

This piston-engine Saab J21A was operated by the Royal Swedish Air Force's Flygflottilj 9.

armament, a pilot's ejection seat, and a twin-boom pusher layout. The first of three J21 prototypes flew in July 1943, with 54 J21A-1 fighters being delivered from December 1945, followed by 124 J21A-2s, which had a revised armament, and 119 J21A-3 fighter-bombers. The conversion to jet power was straightforward: the tailplane was carried high on altered fins and the landing gear was shortened; power was provided by a single de Havilland Goblin 2 turbojet (J21RA), and later with a license-built version of the same engine (J21RB). Thirty of each type were built and after a short career as fighter aircraft, they were converted to attack aircraft and redesignated A21R and A21RB respectively.

Heinkel He 162 Salamander

The He 162 was an innovative design and handled well, but the glue bonding its wooden structure was less than adequate and there were many accidents.

COUNTRY OF ORIGIN: Germany

TYPE: single-seat jet interceptor

POWERPLANT: one 1764 lb (800 kg) BMW 003A-1 turbojet

PERFORMANCE: maximum speed at 19,685 ft (6000 m) 522 mph (840 km/h); service ceiling 39,500 ft (12,040 m); endurance 57 minutes at 35,990 ft (10,970 m)

WEIGHTS: empty 4250 lb (2050 kg); maximum take-off 5941 lb (2695 kg)

DIMENSIONS: wingspan 23 ft 7.5 in (7.20 m); length 29 ft 8.25 in (9.05 m); height 8 ft 4.25 in (2.55 m); wing area 120.56 sq ft (11.20 sq m)

ARMAMENT: two .787 in (20 mm) MG151/20 cannons

The He 162 was a good design aerodynamically, and could be flown by pilots who had very little experience.

Popularly known as the "Volksjäger" (People's Fighter), the He 162 was designed and produced by the war-torn German aviation industry in only six months. With experienced aircrew, fuel and materials in desperately short supply, this marks an incredible achievement.

Specific fighter required

On September 8, 1944, the Reichsluftfahrtsministerium issued a specification calling for a 466 mph (750 km/h) fighter to be ready by January 1, 1945. Huge numbers of workers were seconded to the project and a rapid training program for the Hitler Youth was mounted, using mainly glider aircraft. Heinkel, which had built the

The He 162 Salamander was just becoming operational with LG.1 at the end of the war in Europe. Allied pilots encountered it only rarely.

world's first turbojet aircraft, the He 178, won the design competition with a tiny wooden machine with an engine perched on top. The first prototype flew on December 6, 1944, and deliveries began in January 1945. Thirty prototypes were built, followed by 275 production He 162A-1s/2s, and following trials with Erprobungskommando 162 at Rechlin, the type was issued to I/JG 1 at Leck in Schleswig-Holstein, but this unit did not become operational before the end of the war. Few contacts were made with Allied aircraft, but an unidentified aircraft claimed by a Hawker Tempest pilot of No. 222 Squadron RAF on April 19, 1945, was almost certainly an He 162.

Lockheed P-80 Shooting Star

America's first fully-operational jet fighter, the Lockheed P-80 Shooting Star was very conventional in design. It was to become the workhorse of the US tactical fighter-bomber and fighter interceptor squadrons after WWII.

COUNTRY OF ORIGIN: USA

TYPE: single-seat fighter-bomber

POWERPLANT: one 3850 lb (1746 kg) Allison J33-GE-11 turbojet

PERFORMANCE: maximum speed at sea level 594 mph (966 km/h); service ceiling 46,800 ft (14,265 m); range 825 miles (1328 km)

WEIGHTS: empty 8420 lb (3819 kg); maximum take-off 16,856 lb (7646 kg)

DIMENSIONS: span 38 ft 9 in (11.81 m); length 34 ft 5 in (10.49 m); height 11 ft 3 in (3.43 m); wing area 237.6 sq ft (22.07 sq m)

ARMAMENT: six .5 in (12.7 mm) machine guns, plus two 1000 lb (454 kg) bombs and eight rockets

A neat formation of Lockheed F-80C Shooting Stars. The type was the USAF's tactical "workhorse" of the Korean War.

The prototype XP-80 was designed around a de Havilland H-1 turbojet, supplied to the US in July 1943. The aircraft was completed in just 143 days, making its first flight on January 9, 1944. Early production P-80As entered USAAF service late in 1945 with the 412th Fighter Group. The P-80A was followed by the P-80B; the major production version was the F-80C (the P for "pursuit" prefix having changed to the much more logical F for "fighter").

Shooting down Ilyushin Il-10s

The F-80C was the fighter-bomber workhorse of the Korean War, flying 15,100 sorties in the first four months alone. Pilots found the aircraft ideal for strafing, but the F-80 was rarely able to out-maneuver North Korea's piston-engined Yakovlev and Lavochkin fighters, nor were the US jets initially equipped to carry bombs or rockets for

effective ground-attack work. In spite of these deficiencies, F-80s managed to claim a number of North Korean aircraft. The engagement took place while the F-80s were protecting a flight of North American Twin Mustangs. Captain Raymond E. Schillereff led four aircraft into the Seoul area and caught a quartet of Ilyushin Il-10s interfering with US transport aircraft embarking civilians at Kimpo airfield; all four Il-10s were shot down. The Shooting Star was assured of its place in history when 1st Lt. Russell Brown of the 51st Fighter Wing shot down a MiG-15 jet fighter on November 8, 1950, in a jet-versus-jet battle. Other sporadic attacks were to follow during the early part of the war, until the arrival of the F-86A Sabre.

The USAF's Shooting Stars were not usually camouflaged, appearing mostly in natural metal finish.

Mikoyan-Gurevich MiG-9 "Fargo"

Development of the MiG-9, the USSR's second jet fighter, was initiated in February 1945, the aircraft initially known as the I-300. The prototype flew on April 24, 1946, powered by two BMW 003 turbojets.

COUNTRY OF ORIGIN: USSR

TYPE: Single-seater jet fighter

POWERPLANT: two 1746 lb (800 kg) thrust RD-20 (BMW 003A) turbojet engines

PERFORMANCE: max speed 566 mph (911 km/h); range 900 miles (1448 km) with underwing tanks; service ceiling 44,290 ft (13,500 m)

DIMENSIONS: span 32 ft 10 in (10 m); length 32 ft (9.75 m); height 13 ft (3.96 m)

WEIGHT: 11,177 lb (5070 kg) loaded

ARMAMENT: one 1.46 in (37 mm) and two .90 in (23 mm) cannons

Although heavy and unwieldy, the MiG-9 gave a generation of Soviet pilots their first taste of a jet-combat type.

The prototype of the MiG-9 first flew on April 24, 1946, powered by two BMW 003 turbojets. A small series production batch was built, deliveries to the Soviet Air Force beginning in December 1946.

First Soviet tricycle undercarriage

Early in 1947, production MiG-9s were fitted with the uprated RD-21 engine and redesignated MiG-9F. The last batch of production aircraft had pressurized cockpits and carried the designation MiG-9FR. About 550 aircraft were built in total, including a two-seat trainer variant, the MiG-9UTI. The MiG-9 featured the first tricycle undercarriage installed on a Soviet-built aircraft, the

narrow-track mainwheels retracting outward into the wings. A month after the aircraft's first flight, test pilot Alexander Grinchik was carrying out a high-speed, low-level run in the first prototype when the aircraft suddenly developed an uncontrollable pitch and dived into the ground, killing its pilot. His successor, Mark Gallai, almost came to grief in similar fashion when, during a high-speed run at Mach .8, the nose of the aircraft pitched down violently. The pilot reduced power and managed to restore full control, and after landing it was found that both the tailplane and elevator had become distorted. In all probability Gallai had experienced, but survived, the same problem that had killed his colleague Grinchik.

The MiG-9FR with a pressurized cockpit followed the basic MiG-9 into service and was produced up to the end of 1948.

Republic F-84 Thunderjet

The Republic F-84 Thunderjet began life in the summer of 1944, when Republic Aviation's design team investigated the possibility of adapting the airframe of the P-47 Thunderbolt to take an axial-flow turbojet.

COUNTRY OF ORIGIN: USA

TYPE: single-seat fighter-bomber

POWERPLANT: one 5600 lb (2542 kg) Wright J65-A-29 turbojet

PERFORMANCE: maximum speed 605 mph (973 km/h) at 4,000 ft (1220 m); service ceiling 40,500 ft (12,353 m); combat radius with drop tanks 1000 miles (1609 km)

WEIGHTS: empty 11,460 lb (5203 kg); maximum take-off 28,000 lb (12,701 kg)

DIMENSIONS: span 36 ft 4 in (11.05 m); length 38 ft 5 in (11.71 m); height 12 ft 10 in (3.9 m); wing area 260 sq ft (24.18 sq m)

ARMAMENT: six .5 in (12.7 mm) Browning M3 machine guns, external hardpoints with provision for up to 4000 lb (1814 kg) of stores including rockets and bombs

The Republic F-84 Thunderjet was the first tactical aircraft in the world capable of delivering nuclear weapons.

In November 1944 the design of an entirely new airframe was begun around the General Electric J35 engine. The first of three XP-84 prototypes was completed in December 1945 and made its first flight on February 28, 1946. Three prototypes were followed by 15 YP-84As for the USAF. Delivered in the spring of 1947, they were later converted to F-84B standard. The F-84B was the first production model, featuring an ejection seat, six .5 in (12.7 mm) M3 machine guns and underwing rocket racks.

Outclassed as a fighter

Deliveries of the F-84B began in the summer of 1947 to the 14th Fighter Group, and 226 were built. The F-84C, of which 191 were built, incorporated an improved electrical system and an improved bomb-release mechanism. The next model to appear was the F-84D (151 built). It had a strengthened wing and a modified fuel system. It was followed, in May 1949, by the F-84E, which in addition to its six .5 in (12.7 mm) machine guns could carry two 1000 lb (453 kg) bombs, or 32 rockets. The F-84G, appearing in 1952, was the first Thunderjet variant to be equipped for flight refuelling from the outset. It was also the first USAF fighter to have a tactical nuclear capability. The Thunderjet was widely used during the Korean War. Completely outclassed as a fighter by the MiG-15, it was effective in the ground-attack role. The F-84G appeared in Korea in 1952, and Thunderjets carried out heavy attacks on North Korea's irrigation dams.

The Republic F-84 Thunderjet was first developed as an escort fighter for the US Strategic Air Command.

North American FJ-1 Fury

Although it had a relatively undistinguished career, the North American FJ-1 was the first jet aircraft to complete an operational tour at sea, and for a brief period it could also claim to be the fastest aircraft in US Navy service.

COUNTRY OF ORIGIN: USA

TYPE: single-seat carrierborne fighter

POWERPLANT: one 4000 lb (1816 kg) Allison J35-A-2 turbojet

PERFORMANCE: maximum speed at 9000 ft (2743 m) 547 mph (880 km/h); service ceiling 32,000 ft (9754 m); range 1500 miles (2414 km)

WEIGHTS: empty 8843 lb (4011 kg); maximum loaded 15,600 lb (7076 kg)

DIMENSIONS: span 38 ft 2 in (9.8 m); length 34 ft 5 in (10.5 m); height 14 ft 10 in (4.5 m); wing area 221 sq ft (20.5 sq m)

ARMAMENT: six .5 in (12.7 mm) machine guns

The FJ-1 Fury was not a distinguished fighter, but a land-based version was developed into the excellent F-86 Sabre.

In 1944, before German advanced aeronautical research data was available, the USAAF issued specifications drawn up around four different fighter requirements, the first of which involved a medium-range day-fighter that could also serve in the ground-attack and bomber-escort roles.

Carrierborne jet fighters

This awakened the interest of North American Aviation, whose design team was then working on the NA-134, a projected carrierborne jet fighter for the US Navy. On May 18, 1945, 100 NA-141s (production developments of the NA-134 naval jet fighter under development by North American) were ordered for the US Navy as FJ-1s, (the order was later reduced to 30). Known as the Fury, the FJ-1 first flew November 27, 1946, and went on to serve with Navy Fighter Squadron VF-51, staying in service until 1949. The FJ-1 was the first US carrier jet fighter to be deployed in squadron strength. The NA-134 had a straight-wing design and was well advanced, so North American offered a land-based version to the USAAF under the designation NA-140. On May 18, 1945, North American received a contract for the building of three NA-140 prototypes under the USAAF designation XP-86. These were later fitted with swept flying surfaces, and the incomparable F-86 Sabre was born.

The only squadron to use the FJ-1 was VF-51, its aircraft camouflaged in "midnight blue" paintwork as seen here.

Mikoyan-Gurevich MiG-15

One of the most famous jet fighters of all time, and most outstanding combat aircraft of the post-war years, the MiG-15 was designed by a Russo-German team headed by Artem I. Mikoyan and Mikhail I. Gurevich.

COUNTRY OF ORIGIN: USSR

TYPE: single-seat fighter

POWERPLANT: one 5952 lb (2700 kg) Klimov VK-1 turbojet

PERFORMANCE: maximum speed 684 mph (1100 km/h); service ceiling 51,000 ft (15,545 m); range at height with slipper tanks 885 miles (1424 km)

WEIGHTS: empty 8820 lb (4000 kg); maximum loaded 12,566 lb (5700 kg)

DIMENSIONS: span 33 ft 0.75 in (10.08 m); length 36 ft 3.75 in (11.05 m); height 11 ft 1.75 in (3.4 m); wing area 221.74 sq ft (20.60 sq m)

ARMAMENT: one 1.46 in (37 mm) N-37 cannon and two .91 in (23 mm) NS-23 cannon, plus up to 1102 lb (500 kg) of mixed stores on underwing pylons

As well as serving in huge numbers with the Soviet Air Force, the MiG-15 was one of the most widely exported aircraft in aviation history.

No aircraft in history has had a bigger impact on the world scene than the MiG-15. Its existence was unsuspected in the West until US fighter pilots found themselves confronted by all-swept silver fighters that could fly faster, climb and dive faster, and turn more tightly.

Finding a suitable engine
The aircraft's development could be traced back to a post-war British government decision to send the Soviet Union the latest British turbojet, the Rolls-Royce Nene, long before it was in service with any British service

One of the countries supplied with the MiG-15 was Iraq. This MiG-15UTI trainer is in Iraqi colors.

aircraft. This removed Mikoyan's problem of finding a suitable engine and by the end of December 1947 the prototype was flying, powered by an unlicensed version of the Nene. The MiG-15 saw a great deal of action in its heyday, starting with the Korean War, where it fought the North American F-86 Sabre in the first jet-versus-jet air battles. It also took part in various Arab-Israeli conflicts, serving with Syria and Egypt, and was used operationally over North Vietnam and in the Nigerian civil war. In action over Korea the MiG had a better acceleration, rate of climb and operational ceiling than the F-86 Sabre, but it was a poor gun platform at high speed, being prone to "snaking," and it could be out-turned by the US fighter.

Hawker Sea Hawk

The Hawker Sea Hawk was the Royal Navy's first really viable jet fighter-bomber, and was originally intended for the RAF.

Hawker Sea Hawks, wings folded, on the flight deck of an aircraft carrier, with the crew "dressing ship" in the background.

COUNTRY OF ORIGIN: United Kingdom

TYPE: single-seat carrier-based fighter-bomber

POWERPLANT: one 5000 lb (2268 kg) Rolls-Royce Nene turbojet

PERFORMANCE: maximum speed at sea level 599 mph (958 km/h); or 587 mph (939 km/h) at height; service ceiling 44,500 ft (13,560 m); standard range 740 miles (1191 km)

WEIGHTS: empty 9720 lb (4409 kg); maximum take-off 16,200 lb (7355 kg)

DIMENSIONS: span 39 ft (11.89 m); length 39 ft 8 in (12.09 m); height 8 ft 8 in (2.64 m); wing area 278 sq ft (25.83 sq m)

ARMAMENT: four .787 in (20 mm) Hispano cannons in nose, underwing hardpoints for two 500 lb (227 kg) bombs

The Royal Netherlands Navy was a major user of the Sea Hawk, operating the type from its carrier the *Karel Doormand*.

The Sea Hawk was legendary Hawker designer Sir Sidney Camm's first jet fighter. The first flight of the initial prototype took place on September 2, 1947. The Royal Navy ordered 151 of the navalized version fitted with carrier equipment and with the wing span increased by 2 ft 6 in (.9 m). Hawker Siddeley built only 35 of these F.1s; all subsequent design and production was handled by Armstrong Whitworth of Coventry.

Finding a suitable engine

The F.2 featured powered ailerons, and the FB.3 was fitted with underwing racks to permit the carriage of two bombs or mines. The FB. Mk 3 also had a strengthened main wing spar to accommodate the increased weapon load. In total 116 of the FB.Mk 3s were delivered to the Royal Navy. Many were later converted to FB. Mk 5 standard by fitting a more powerful 5400 lb (2449 kg) Rolls-Royce Nene 103. Sea Hawks were issued to Fleet Air Arm squadrons in 1953, and three years later the type saw action with six squadrons during the Suez crisis, carrying out many ground-attack operations. Sea Hawks also served with the Royal Netherlands Navy, the Federal German Naval Air Arm, and the Indian Navy. The latter's Sea Hawks saw brief combat in 1971, supporting the Indian Army's invasion of Bangladesh.

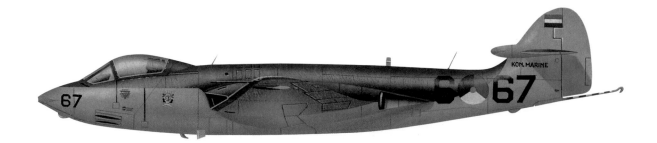

North American F-86 Sabre

Thanks to its excellent performance in combat during the Korean War, the North American F-86 Sabre quickly became a combat legend, and was NATO's main interceptor type in the early 1950s.

COUNTRY OF ORIGIN: USA	
TYPE: Single-seater interceptor	
POWERPLANT: one 5200 lb (235 kg) thrust General Electric J47-GE-13 turbojet engine	
PERFORMANCE: maximum speed 675 mph (1086 km/h); range 783 miles (1260 km); service ceiling 48,300 ft (14,720 m)	
DIMENSIONS: span 37 ft 1 in (11.30 m); length 37 ft 6 in (11.43 m); height 14 ft 8 in (4.47 m)	
WEIGHT: loaded 14,720 lb (6675 kg)	
ARMAMENT: six .5 in (12.7 mm) Colt-Browning machine guns; up to 2000 lb (907 kg) of underwing stores	

This front view of an F-86A Sabre shows the aircraft's air intake configuration and the three .5 in (12.7 mm) guns on either side of the nose.

The first of two XF-86 prototypes flew on August 8, 1947, powered by a General Electric J35 turbojet. The second prototype, the XF-86A, made its first flight on May 18, 1948, fitted with a General Electric J-47-GE-1 engine. Deliveries of production F-86As began ten days later. The first operational F-86As were delivered to the 1st Fighter Group early in 1949. On March 4, 1949, the North American F-86 was officially named the Sabre. Production of the F-86A ended with the 554th aircraft in December 1950.

Destroyer of MiG-15s
During the next two and a half years, Sabres were to destroy 810 enemy aircraft, 792 of them MiG-15s. The next Sabre variants were the F-86C penetration fighter (redesignated YF-93A), which flew only as a prototype, and the F-86D all-weather fighter, which had a complex fire-control system and a ventral rocket pack; 2201 were built, the F-86L being an updated version. The F-86E was an F-86A with power-operated controls and an all-flying tail; 396 were built before the variant was replaced by the F-86F, the major production version with 2247 examples being delivered. The F-86H was a specialized fighter-bomber armed with four .787 in (20 mm) cannons and carrying a tactical nuclear weapon; the F-86K was a simplified F-86D; and the designation F-86J was applied to the Canadair-built Sabre Mk.3. Most Sabres built by Canadair were destined for NATO air forces; the RAF, for example, received 427 Sabre Mk.4s. The Sabre Mk.6 was the last variant built by Canadair. It was also built under license in Australia as the Sabre Mk.30/32. The total number of Sabres built by North American, Fiat and Mitsubishi was 6208, with 1815 more built by Canadair.

This F-86 Sabre has ten red stars, denoting enemy aircraft destroyed over Korea. Sabre pilots' claims were later greatly revised.

McDonnell F2H Banshee

The F2H Banshee stemmed from a 1945 US Navy requirement for a jet fighter-bomber. The prototype, designated XF2D-1, flew for the first time on January 11, 1947, powered by two Westinghouse J34 turbojets.

COUNTRY OF ORIGIN: USA

TYPE: carrier-based all-weather fighter

POWERPLANT: one 3250 lb (1474 kg) Westinghouse J34-WE-34 turbojet

PERFORMANCE: maximum cruising speed 580 mph (933 km/h); service ceiling 46,600 ft (14,205 m); combat range 1170 miles (1883 km)

WEIGHTS: empty 13,183 lb (5980 kg); maximum take-off 25,214 lb (11,437 kg)

DIMENSIONS: span 41 ft 9 in (12.73 m); length 48 ft 2 in (14.68 m); height 14 ft 6 in (4.42 m); wing area 294 sq ft (27.31 sq m)

ARMAMENT: four .787 in (20 mm) cannons; underwing racks with provision for two 500 lb (227 kg) or four 250 lb (113 kg) bombs

The F2H Banshee was an effective combat aircraft, but somewhat inferior to the Grumman F9F Panther in the ground-attack role.

The success of the FH-1 Phantom in operational service meant it was almost inevitable that McDonnell was to submit a design to succeed the Phantom in service. The Banshee design team under G.V. Covington kept to a broadly similar configuration to the aircraft's predecessor, with a low mid-set unswept wing and tricycle landing gear. The new aircraft was larger, with folding wings and a lengthened fuselage to accommodate more fuel, and more powerful engines in fattened wing roots. The aircraft was initially designated F-2D, later F2H, and finally F-2. The first F2H-1 aircraft was delivered to the Navy in August 1948, and was followed into service by seven sub-variants. Almost all of the aircraft saw service in Korea, in a wide variety of roles. The F2H-2 was the second production version, with wingtip fuel tanks. Production total was 56.

First combat

The Banshee went into combat in Korea for the first time on August 23, 1951, when F2H-2s of VF-172 (USS *Essex*) struck at targets in northwest Korea. The F2H-2P was a photo-reconnaissance variant (89 built). The F2H-3 (redesignated F2-C in 1962) was a long-range limited all-weather development (250 built), and the type equipped two squadrons of the Royal Canadian Navy, operating from the carrier HMCS *Bonaventure*.

This F2H Banshee of Marine squadron VNJ-1 was the veteran of many attack missions, as shown by the markings under its cockpit.

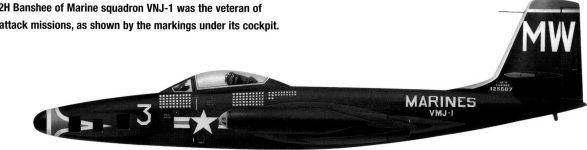

Chance Vought F7U Cutlass

The radical Chance Vought F7U Cutlass had several claims to fame. It was the first production naval aircraft to achieve supersonic flight and the first to release bombs at supersonic speed.

Because of the Cutlass's very long nosewheel leg, the cockpit was at a considerable height from the ground.

COUNTRY OF ORIGIN: USA

TYPE: carrier-based fighter-bomber

POWERPLANT: two 4200 lb (1905kg) Westinghouse J34-32 turbojets

PERFORMANCE: maximum speed at sea level 665 mph (1070 km/h); service ceiling 41,000 ft (12,500 m); combat radius with maximum fuel 600 miles (966 km)

WEIGHTS: empty 5385kg (11,870lb); maximum take-off 7640kg (16,840lb)

DIMENSIONS: span 38 ft 8 in (11.78 m); length 39 ft 7 in (12.07 m); height 9 ft 10 in (3 m); wing area 496 sq ft (46.08 sq m)

ARMAMENT: four .787 in (20 mm) M-2 cannons

The Cutlass was designed in 1946, when fighter aerodynamics had been thrown into turmoil by wartime German research and emerging jet technology. The design incorporated a 38-degree swept wing carrying wide-span powered elevons, airbrakes and full-span leading-edge slats. Twin vertical tails were mounted at one-third span.

Ahead of its time

These features were remarkably advanced for the time, as was the use of afterburning engines, an automatic stabilization system, and controls with artificial feedback. Three prototype XF7U-1s were built, and the first of these flew on September 29, 1949. The performance of the F7U-1 fell short of USN requirements and production was halted after 14 aircraft to enable modifications. The aircraft re-emerged as the F7U-3, which entered service in April 1954. The F7U-3M was armed with four Sparrow AAMs, while the F7U-3P was a photo-reconnaissance version. Production totalled 307 F7U-3s, 98 F7U-3Ms and 12 F7U-3Ps. The F7U had a high accident rate and was loathed by its pilots, who nicknamed it the "Gutless."

The F7U Cutlass was intended to be a great leap forward, but its innovative nature was its downfall and it never made the grade.

Dassault MD.450 Ouragan

For the first few years after WWII, the French Air Force relied on foreign jet aircraft for its first-line equipment, but in February 1949 Avions Marcel Dassault flew the prototype of a straightforward, no-frills jet fighter.

COUNTRY OF ORIGIN: France

TYPE: single-seat fighter/ground attack aircraft

POWERPLANT: one 5070 lb (2300 kg) Hispano-Suiza Nene 104B turbojet

PERFORMANCE: maximum speed 584 mph (940 km/h); service ceiling 49,210 ft (15,000 m); range 620 miles (1000 km)

WEIGHTS: empty 9150 lb (4150 kg); maximum take-off 17,416 lb (7600 kg)

DIMENSIONS: span over tip tanks 43 ft 2 in (13.2 m); length 35 ft 3 in (10.74 m); height 13 ft 7 in (4.15 m); wing area 256.18 sq ft (23.8 sq m)

ARMAMENT: four .787 in (20 mm) Hispano 404 cannons; underwing hardpoints for two 1000 lb (434 kg) bombs, or 16 4.134 in (105 mm) rockets, or eight rockets and two 101 ga (458 liter) napalm tanks

A simple and robust jet fighter, the Ouragan gave France's military aircraft industry a much-needed boost.

World War II destroyed the French aircraft industry, and it had to be rebuilt from scratch while learning the new technology of jet propulsion. Most companies in the newly nationalized French aviation industry failed to see any of their designs built in any quantity.

Destroyer of MiG-15s
However, the private firm of Dassault produced one of the most enduring, successful families of combat aircraft in the world. The whole line of Mirages, Etendards, Mystères and Rafales stem from the simple, conventional, but highly effective Ouragan (Hurricane) of 1949. Powered by a license-built version of the British Rolls-Royce Nene turbojet, the first unarmed prototype was flown in February 1949. Equipped with a pressurized cockpit and wingtip fuel tanks, the first of 150 production aircraft entered service in 1952. The Ouragan was exported to India, where it was known as the Toofani (Whirlwind), and 75 examples went to Israel. The Ouragan was inferior to the MiG-15, the jet-fighter type then equipping the Egyptian Air Force, it performed well in the ground-attack role. Indian Air Force Ouragans saw combat in the various Indo-Pakistan conflicts, while the Israeli aircraft saw much action in the Arab-Israeli wars of 1956 and 1967.

This Israeli Air Force Ouragan carries the identification stripes used by Israeli, British and French aircraft during the Suez campaign of 1956.

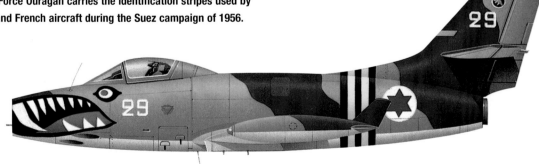

Mikoyan-Gurevich MiG-17 "Fresco"

When the MiG-17 first appeared in the early 1950s, Western observers at first believed that it was an improved MiG-15, with new features that reflected the technical lessons learned during the Korean War. They were wrong.

COUNTRY OF ORIGIN: USSR

TYPE: single-seat fighter

POWERPLANT: one 7452 lb (3383 kg) Klimov VK-1F turbojet

PERFORMANCE: maximum speed at 9,840 ft (3000 m) 711 mph (1145 km/h); service ceiling 54,560 ft (16,600 m); range at height with slipper tanks 913 miles (1470 km)

WEIGHTS: empty 9040 lb (4100 kg); maximum loaded 14,770 lb (6000 kg)

DIMENSIONS: span 31 ft (9.45 m); length 36 ft 3.75 in (11.05 m); height 11 ft (3.35 m); wing area 221.74 sq ft (20.60 sq m)

ARMAMENT: one 1.46 in (37 mm) N-37 cannon and two .91 in (23 mm) NS-23 cannon, plus up to 1102 lb (500 kg) of mixed stores on underwing pylons

The MiG-17UTI, seen here, was the two-seat trainer variant of the jet fighter.

In fact, design of the MiG-17 had begun in 1949, the new type incorporating a number of aerodynamic refinements that included a new tail on a longer fuselage and a thinner wing and three boundary layer fences to improve handling at high speed. The basic version, known to NATO as Fresco-A, entered service in 1952; this was followed by the MiG-17P all-weather interceptor (Fresco-B) and then the major production variant, the MiG-17F (Fresco-C), which was fitted with an afterburner.

Historical importance

The last variant, the MiG-17PFU, was armed with air-to-air missiles. Full-scale production of the MiG-17 in the

The MiG-17 was widely exported, and was offered to some countries at cut-rate prices. This is an Indonesian Air Force example.

Soviet Union lasted only five years before the type was superseded by the supersonic MiG-19 and MiG-21, but around 8800 were built in that time, of which some 5000 were MiG-17Fs. MiG-17s saw action in the Congo, in the Nigerian civil war and in the Middle East, where they were the workhorse fighter-bombers of the Syrian Air Force. Some were fitted with six underwing hardpoints, as on the license-built Polish version. The MiG-17's claim to historical importance rests on its use by North Vietnamese Air Force (NVAF) units from 1965–73. The MIG-17 had a far lower wing loading than its opponents; its span was almost as great as that of the F-4 Phantom, but its loaded weight was about the same as that of the F-4's internal fuel load. The result was that the MiG-17 could enter a relatively slow but very tight turn that no US aircraft could match.

Republic F-84F Thunderstreak

The F-84F gave many NATO air forces their first experience of fast, low-level ground-attack-jet combat flying. It was a straightforward swept-wing development of the F-84 Thunderjet.

An F-84F Thunderstreak launching a GAM-83 Bullpup air-to-surface missile during trials.

The swept-wing XF-84F Thunderstreak first flew on June 3, 1950, only 167 days after it was ordered. The first production F-84F flew on November 22, 1952, and the type was officially accepted by the USAF in the following month.

Modern, swept-wing jet aircraft

The first USAF unit to arm with the F-84F, in 1954, was the 407th Tactical Fighter Wing. The F-84F replaced the Thunderjet in several NATO air forces, giving many European pilots their first experience of modern, swept-wing jet aircraft. In French Air Force service, it saw action

The F-84F was an important asset in the squadrons of the USAF Tactical Air Command during the mid-1950s.

during the 1956 Anglo-French operation to secure the Suez Canal, flying from a base in Israel to destroy a number of Egyptian Il-28 jet bombers that had been evacuated to Luxor. The RF-84F Thunderflash was a low-level tactical reconnaissance variant. The Thunderstreak equipped the 4th and 9th Escadres of the French Air Force, Nos. 31, 32, 33, 34 and 35 Wings of the Luftwaffe, Gruppi 20, 21, 22, 101, 102, 154, 155 and 165 of the Italian Air Force, the 1st, 2nd, 3rd, 23rd, 27th and 31st Squadrons of the Belgian Air Force, as well as four Royal Netherlands Air Force squadrons, three Greek AF Wings and nine Turkish AF squadrons.

COUNTRY OF ORIGIN: USA

TYPE: single-seat fighter-bomber

POWERPLANT: one 7220 lb (3278 kg) Wright J65-W-3 turbojet

PERFORMANCE: maximum speed 695 mph (1118 km/h); service ceiling 46,000 ft (14,020 kg); combat radius with drop tanks 810 miles (1304 km)

WEIGHTS: empty 13,830 lb (6273 kg); maximum take-off 28,000 lb (12,701 kg)

DIMENSIONS: span 33 ft 7.25 in (10.24 m); length 43 ft 4.75 in (13.23 m); height 14 ft 4.75 in (4.39 m); wing area 325 sq ft (30.19 sq m)

ARMAMENT: six .5 in (12.7 mm) Browning M3 machine guns, external hardpoints with provision for up to 6000 lb (2722 kg) of stores

Douglas F4D Skyray

The design of the Douglas F4D Skyray, which first flew on January 23, 1951, owed much to the wartime work of Dr. Alexander Lippisch, whose delta-wing designs had made an impression on the US Navy's Bureau of Aeronautics.

COUNTRY OF ORIGIN: USA

TYPE: single-seat carrier-based fighter

POWERPLANT: one 10,200 lb (4626 kg) Pratt & Whitney J57-P-8A turbojet

PERFORMANCE: maximum speed at 36,000 ft (10,975 m) 695 mph (1162 km/h); service ceiling above 55,000 ft (16,765 m); range 1,200 miles (1931 km)

WEIGHTS: empty 16,024 lb (7268 kg); maximum take-off 25,000 lb (11,340 kg)

DIMENSIONS: span 33 ft 6 in (10.21 m); length 45 ft 8.25 in (13.93 m); height 13 ft (3.96 m); wing area 557 sq ft (51.75 sq m)

ARMAMENT: four .787 in (20 mm) cannon; six underwing hardpoints with provision for up to 4000 lb (1814 kg) of stores, including AIM-9C Sidewinder air-to-air missiles, bombs, rockets or drop tanks

The F4D Skyray provided the US Navy and other air arms with a powerful strike capability for many years.

Details of German research into delta wings generated great interest in the US Navy, prompting senior officers to request a design submission from Douglas. This was finalized as a variation on a pure delta-wing configuration in 1948, and Douglas won a contract to build two prototypes that year. The first aircraft made its maiden flight in January 1951 with an Allison turbojet, but continual engine problems during the development program led to the selection of a Pratt & Whitney unit for production aircraft. The design was a cantilever mid-wing monoplane controlled by trailing-edge elevons serving collectively as elevators or differentially as ailerons. The cockpit was situated well forward of the wing and afforded

the pilot excellent all-round visibility. When the first production F4D-1 exceeded Mach One in level flight on June 5, 1954, it seemed probable that the aircraft would soon enter service, but serious problems, including a dangerous high-speed stall at altitude, had to be overcome before the aircraft could be deployed operationally in 1956.

Time-to-height records

Production of the Skyray ended in 1958 with the 419th aircraft, but the type remained in first-line service until well into the 1960s. During its operational career the Skyray established five new time-to-height records.

This is a Douglas F4D-1 Skyray of VF-162 "The Hunters," which was based on the USS Intrepid, in the Mediterranean from 1961-62.

Supermarine Swift

Together with the Hawker Hunter, the Supermarine Swift was intended to replace the Meteor in the air-defense role within RAF Fighter Command. Both types were ordered into "super-priority" production.

Designed by a Supermarine team that had cut its teeth on the Spitfire and the Attacker, the Swift had a problematic development, matched by an unfulfilled service life. The prototype 541 Swift was deficient in many respects and spring-tab ailerons prohibited supersonic dives. Later geared-tab surfaces made transonic flight possible, but control was poor about all axes and dangerous above 25,000 ft (7620 m). The Swift F.Mk.1, however, was found to be unsuitable for its primary role of high-level interception, being prone to tightening in turns and suffering frequent high-altitude flameouts as a result of

One of the prototype Swifts, this aircraft starred in the 1950s film *The Sound Barrier*.

COUNTRY OF ORIGIN: United Kingdom

TYPE: single-seat tactical reconnaissance aircraft

POWERPLANT: one 9450 lb (4287 kg) Rolls-Royce Avon 114 turbojet

PERFORMANCE: maximum speed 685 mph (1100 km/h); service ceiling 45,800 ft (13,690 m); range 630 miles (1014 km)

WEIGHTS: empty 12,800 lb (5800 kg); maximum take-off 21,400 lb (9,706 kg)

DIMENSIONS: span 32 ft 4 in (9.85 m); length 42 ft 3 in (12.88 m); height 12 ft 6 in (3.8 m); wing area 485 sq ft (45.06 sq m)

ARMAMENT: two 1.18 in (30 mm) Aden cannon plus provision for underwing rockets and bombs

shock waves entering the air intakes when the cannon were fired. These problems were largely rectified in the Swift F.Mk.4, but only four of these were built.

Low-level tactical reconnaissance

It was adapted to the low-level fighter reconnaissance role, with three cameras installed in a lengthened nose. Sixty-two Swift FR.Mk.5s were produced, 35 being converted from Swift F.Mk.4 airframes. The Swift FR.5 performed extremely well in the low-level tactical reconnaissance role, being eventually replaced by the Hunter FR.10.

This is a Swift FR.5 in the markings of No. 79 Squadron, 2nd Allied Tactical Air Force, Gütersloh, Germany.

WK 293

Hawker Hunter

The most successful post-war British fighter aircraft, the Hunter has an elegance that matches its effectiveness. It is fondly remembered by a generation of pilots who delighted in its superb handling characteristics.

COUNTRY OF ORIGIN: United Kingdom

TYPE: single-seat fighter

POWERPLANT: one 6500 lb (2925 kg) Rolls-Royce Avon 100 turbojet

PERFORMANCE: maximum speed at sea level 710 mph (1144 km/h); service ceiling 50,000 ft (15,240 m); range on internal fuel 490 miles (689 km)

WEIGHTS: empty 12,128 lb (5501 kg); loaded 16,200 lb (7347 kg)

DIMENSIONS: span 33 ft 8 in (10.26 m); length 45 ft 10.5 in (13.98 m); height 13 ft 2 in (4.02 m); wing area 349 sq ft (32.42 sq m)

ARMAMENT: four 1.18 in (30 mm) Aden cannons; underwing pylons with provision for two 1000 lb (453.6 kg) bombs and 24 3 in (76.2 mm) rockets

Swiss Air Force Hunters frequently practiced operating from stretches of autobahn, as seen here.

The Hunter F.Mk.1, which entered service early in 1954, suffered from engine-surge problems during high-altitude gun-firing trials, resulting in some modifications to its Rolls-Royce Avon turbojet, and this led to the Hunter F4, which gradually replaced the Canadair-built F-86E Sabre (which had been supplied to the RAF as an interim fighter) in the German-based squadrons of the 2nd Tactical Air Force. The Hunter Mks 2 and 5 were variants powered by the Armstrong Siddeley Sapphire engine.

Widely exported

In 1953 Hawker equipped the Hunter with the large 10,000 lb (4535 kg) thrust Avon 203 engine, and this variant, designated Hunter F.Mk.6, flew for the first time in January 1954. Deliveries began in 1956 and the F6 subsequently equipped 15 squadrons of RAF Fighter Command. The Hunter FGA.9 was a development of the F6 optimized for ground attack, as its designation implies. The Hunter Mks 7, 8, 12, T52, T62, T66, T67 and T69 were all two-seat trainer variants, while the FR.10 was a fighter-reconnaissance version, converted from the F.6. The GA.11 was an operational trainer for the Royal Navy. The Hunter was widely exported. The aircraft was license-built in Holland and Belgium; principal customers for British-built aircraft were India, Switzerland and Sweden. Indian Hunters saw considerable action in the 1965 and 1971 conflicts with Pakistan.

This is a Hunter F.Mk 1 of No. 43 Squadron, which was based at RAF Leuchars, in Scotland, in 1954.

Dassault Mystère IVA

The Dassault Mystère IV was unquestionably one of the finest combat aircraft of its era. Although developed from the Mystère IIC, it was a completely new design. The prototype Mystère IVA first flew in September 1952.

COUNTRY OF ORIGIN: France

TYPE: single-seat fighter bomber

POWERPLANT: one 6,280 lb (2850 kg) Hispano Suiza Tay 250A turbojet; or 7716 lb (3500 kg) Hispano Suiza Verdon 350 turbojet

PERFORMANCE: maximum speed 696 mph (1120 km/h); service ceiling 45,000 ft (13,750 m); range 820 miles (1320 km)

WEIGHTS: empty 11,514 lb (5875 kg); loaded 20,950 lb (9500 kg)

DIMENSIONS: span 36 ft 5.75 in (11.1 m); length 42 ft 2 in (12.9 m); height 14 ft 5 in (4.4 m)

ARMAMENT: two 1.18 in (30 mm) DEFA 551 cannons with 150 rounds, four underwing hardpoints with provision for up to 2000 lb (907 kg) of stores, including tanks, rockets or bombs

The Mystère IVA was in the same category as Britain's Hawker Hunter, and served alongside it in Indian Air Force service.

Although superficially similar to the II series aircraft, the IVA was in fact a completely new aircraft, with hardly a single structural part being common to both. The wing of the IV was thinner, more sharply swept, and much strengthened. The fuselage and tail were completely new and the pilot enjoyed powered controls.

Suez campaign fighter
The US Air Force tested the prototype, which first flew as M.D 454-01 on September 28, 1952, and placed an offshore contract for 225 of the production aircraft in April 1953 to equip the Armée de l'Air. The first

50 production aircraft had the Rolls-Royce Tay engine, but the remainder each had a Hispano Suiza Verdon 350. Israel purchased 60 Mystère IVAs for the air defense role, the first 24 being delivered in May 1956 for service with No. 101 Squadron in time for action in the Sinai (Suez) campaign, in which the type claimed seven kills. Another 36 arrived in August, including one fitted out for reconnaissance, allowing No. 109 Squadron to re-equip in December. The Mystère IVA was also used by India, the type seeing extensive action in the 1965 war against Pakistan.

Israel made extensive use of the Mystère IVA, which enabled it to establish air superiority in the 1956 Sinai campaign.

Saab A/J 32 Lansen

In the autumn of 1946, Saab began design studies of a new turbojet-powered attack aircraft for the Swedish Air Force, and two years later the Swedish Air Board authorized the construction of a prototype designated P1150.

COUNTRY OF ORIGIN: Sweden

TYPE: all-weather and night-fighter

POWERPLANT: one 15,190 lb (6890 kg) Svenska Flygmotor (Rolls-Royce Avon) RM6A

PERFORMANCE: maximum speed 692 mph (1114 km/h); service ceiling 52,500 ft (16,013 m); range with external fuel 2000 miles (3220 km)

WEIGHTS: empty 17,600 lb (7990 kg); maximum loaded 29,800 lb (13,529 kg)

DIMENSIONS: span 42 ft 7.75 in (13 m); length 47 ft 6.75 in (14.50 m); height 15 ft 3 in (4.65 m); wing area 402.58 sq ft (37.4 sq m)

ARMAMENT: four 1.18 in (30 mm) Aden M/55 cannons; four Rb324 (Sidewinder) air-to-air missiles or FFAR (Folding Fin Air-launched Rocket) pods

The Lansen was Sweden's equivalent of Britain's Hawker Hunter, and in fact used the same Rolls-Royce engine as the British fighter.

Designed to replace the Saab 18 light-bomber in service with the Swedish air force, the Type 32 was a large all-swept machine of outstanding quality, designed and developed ahead of similar aircraft elsewhere in Western Europe. Owing to its not inconsiderable size, it was capable of development for three dissimilar missions. Three more prototypes were built, and one of these exceeded Mach One in a shallow dive on October 25, 1953. The A–32A attack variant was followed by the J–32B all-weather fighter, which first flew in January 1957. A two-seater, the J–32B was powered by an RM6 (licence-built RA28) turbojet and carried an improved armament, navigation equipment and fire-control system. The J–37B was very much an interim aircraft, filling a gap until the advent of a much more potent system, the Saab J–35 Draken.

Reconnaisance version

The S–32C was a reconnaissance version. The Lansen equipped seven squadrons at its peak, and served in many other roles, including target tug and trials aircraft, well into the 1990s.

This Lansen is armed with an RB 04E air-to-surface missile, its primary weapon.

Mikoyan-Gurevich MiG-19 "Farmer"

Designed as a successor to the MiG-17, the MiG-19 was the first operational Soviet aircraft capable of exceeding Mach One in level flight.

Two MiG-19s (Shenyang F-6s) of the Pakistan Air Force are flanked in this formation by two MiG-17UTIs.

With the unveiling of the MiG-19 the Mikoyan-Gurevich bureau established itself at the forefront of the world's fighter design teams. The new fighter was in the preliminary design stage before the MiG-15 had been encountered over Korea, with five prototypes ordered in July 1951. The first flew in September 1953, powered by twin AM-5 engines. With afterburning engines the MiG-19 became the first supersonic fighter in Soviet service. The first production model proved to have stability problems, and after modifications a second variant, the MiG-19S, went into service in 1956. Both were known to NATO as Farmer-A.

All-seater fighter variant

In 1958 an all-seater fighter variant, MiG-19P (Farmer-B), appeared, followed by the MiG-19C (Farmer-F). The MiG-19PF was a missile-armed all-weather variant, while the MiG-19PM was a night-fighter. The MiG-19 was built under license in China, Poland and Czechoslovakia. Chinese-built aircraft were exported to Pakistan and Vietnam, seeing combat with both countries' air forces.

COUNTRY OF ORIGIN: USSR

TYPE: single-seat all-weather interceptor

POWERPLANT: two 7165 lb (3250 kg) Klimov RD-9B turbojets

PERFORMANCE: maximum speed at 20,000 ft (9080 m) 920 mph (1480 km/h); service ceiling 58,725 ft (17,900 m); maximum range at high altitude with two drop tanks 1367 miles (2200 km)

WEIGHTS: empty 12,698 lb (5760 kg); maximum take-off 20,944 lb (9500 kg)

DIMENSIONS: span 29 ft 6.5 in (9 m); length 44 ft 7 in (13.58 m); height 13 ft 2.25 in (4.02 m); wing area 269.11 sq ft (25 sq m)

ARMAMENT: underwing pylons for four AA-1 Alkali air-to-air-missiles, or AA-2 Atoll

The MiG-19, seen here in aerobat team colors, was the Soviet Air Force's first truly supersonic fighter.

North American F-100 Super Sabre

Originally known as the Sabre 45, the F-100 bore little resemblance to its predecessor, the F-86, having a contoured low-drag fuselage, and wings and tail surface swept at an angle of 45 degrees.

COUNTRY OF ORIGIN: USA

TYPE: single-seat fighter-bomber

POWERPLANT: one 17,000 lb (7711 kg) Pratt & Whitney J57-P-21A turbojet

PERFORMANCE: maximum speed at 35,000 ft (10,670 m) 864 mph (1390 km/h); service ceiling 46,000 ft (14,020 m); range with internal fuel 600 miles (966 km)

WEIGHTS: empty 21,000 lb (9525 kg); maximum take-off 34,832 lb (15,800 kg)

DIMENSIONS: span 38 ft 9.5 in (11.82 m); length excluding probe 47 ft 1.25 in (14.36 m); height 16 ft 3 in (4.95 m); wing area 385 sq ft (35.77 sq m)

ARMAMENT: four .787 in (20 mm) cannon; eight external hardpoints with provision for two drop tanks and up to 7500 lb (3402 kg) of stores, bombs, cluster bombs, dispenser weapons, rocket-launcher pods, cannon pods and ECM pods

The F-100 Super Sabre was the USAF Tactical Air Command's principal fighter-bomber type until the arrival of the F-4 Phantom.

On November 1, 1951, the USAF awarded a contract for two YF-100A prototypes and 110 F-100A production aircraft; the first prototype flew on May 25, 1953, and exceeded Mach One on its maiden flight. The first F100A Super Sabres were delivered to the 479th Fighter Wing at George AFB, California, in September 1954.

Resolving unexplained crashes

The planes were grounded in November following a series of crashes caused by the vertical tail surfaces being too small to enable pilots to maintain control during certain maneuvers, so they were redesigned with 27 percent more area. The F-100A began flying operationally again in February 1955 and 22 were built. The next series production variant was the F-100C, which was capable of carrying out both ground-attack and interception missions. First deliveries to the USAF were made in July 1955 and total production was 451, of which 260 went to the Turkish Air Force. The F-100D differed from the F-100C in having an automatic pilot, jettisonable underwing pylons and modified vertical tail surfaces; it was supplied to the USAF Tactical Air Command, Denmark, France and Greece. The TF-100C was a two-seat trainer variant and served as the prototype of the TF-100F, which flew in July 1957. Total production of all Super Sabre variants was 2294, many aircraft serving in Vietnam.

An F-100D Super Sabre in the markings used during the early phase of the Vietnam War, before camouflage was adopted.

Lockheed F-104 Starfighter

Development of the F-104 started 1951, when lessons learned in the Korean air war were causing changes in combat aircraft design. A contract for two XF-104 prototypes was placed in 1953. The first flew in February 1954.

The F-104 Starfighter caused a sensation when it first appeared, being much faster than any other fighter then in operational service.

COUNTRY OF ORIGIN: USA

TYPE: single-seat multi-mission strike fighter

POWERPLANT: one 15,600 lb (7076 kg) General Electric J79-GE-11A turbojet

PERFORMANCE: maximum speed at 50,000 ft (15,240 m) 1146 mph (1845 km/h); service ceiling 50,000 ft (15,240 m); range 1081 miles (1740 km)

WEIGHTS: empty 13,995 lb (6348 kg); maximum take-off 29,035 lb (13,170 kg)

DIMENSIONS: wingspan (excluding missiles) 21 ft 9 in (6.36 m); length 54 ft 8 in (16.66 m); height 13 ft 5 in (4.09 m); wing area 196.10 sq ft (18.22 sq m)

ARMAMENT: one .787 in (20 mm) General Electric M61A1 cannon, provision for AIM-9 Sidewinder on fuselage, under wings or on tips, and/or stores up to a maximum of 4000 lb (1814 kg)

The aircraft was ordered into production as the F-104A, deliveries to the USAF Air Defense Command beginning in January 1958. Because it lacked all-weather capability, the F-104A saw only limited service with Air Defense Command, equipping only two figher squadrons. F104As were also supplied to Nationalist China and Pakistan, and saw combat during the Indo–Pakistan conflict of 1969.

Reaching Mach 2.4
The F104B was a two-seat version, and the F-104C was a tactical fighter-bomber, the first of 77 being delivered to the 479th Tactical Fighter Wing in October 1958. Two more two-seat Starfighters, the F-104D and F-104F, were followed by the F-104G single-seat multi-mission aircraft, which was numerically the most important variant. The first F-104G flew on October 5, 1960, and 1266 were built

up to February 1966, 977 by the European Starfighter Consortium and the remainder by Lockheed. Of these, the Luftwaffe received 750, the Italian Air Force 154, the Royal Netherlands Air Force 120 and the Belgian Air Force 99. The basically similar CF-104 was a strike-reconnaissance aircraft, 200 of which were built by Canadair for the RCAF. Canadair also built 110 more F-104Gs for delivery to the air forces of Norway, Nationalist China, Spain, Denmark, Greece and Turkey. Also similar to the F-104G was the F-104J for the Japan Air Self-Defense Force; the first one flew on June 30, 1961, and and 207 were produced by Mitsubishi. The F-104S was an interceptor development of the F-104G, and was capable of Mach 2.4; 165 were license-built in Italy.

For service in Vietnam, the F-104 adopted a two-tone camouflage scheme.

McDonnell F-101 Voodoo

Designed as an escort fighter and long-range interceptor, the McDonnell F-101 Voodoo found a much different application as a tactical strike and reconnaissance aircraft.

COUNTRY OF ORIGIN: USA

TYPE: (F-101A VOODOO) single-seat day ground-attack aircraft

POWERPLANT: two 14,880 lb (6750 kg) Pratt & Whitney J57-P-13 turbojets

PERFORMANCE: maximum speed at 35,000 ft (10,675 m) 1009 mph (1623 km/h); service ceiling 55,800 ft (16,775 m); range 1900 miles (3057 km)

WEIGHTS: empty 24,970 lb (11,336 kg); maximum take-off 52,400 lb (23,768 kg)

DIMENSIONS: span 39 ft 8 in (12.09 m); length 67 ft 4.75 in (20.54 m); height 18 ft (5.49 m); wing area 368 sq ft (34.19 sq m)

ARMAMENT: four .787 in (20 mm) cannon; one centerline pylon with provsion for one MT tactical nuclear bomb and two wing pylons for two 2000 lb (907 kg) conventional bombs, or four 680 lb (310 kg) mines, or other ordnance

The F-101 Voodoo had a long gestation period, starting life as the XF-88 long-range escort-fighter project.

Originally intended as a long-range escort for Strategic Air Command, the early F-101A prototypes proved to have inadequate range and so the aircraft was adopted by Tactical Air Command as an attack aircraft. The first F-101A was flown in September 1954, and service delivery began in early 1957 with the 27th Tactical Fighter Wing at Bergstrom, Texas. At this time they were the heaviest and most powerful single-seat fighter in Air Force service. Fifty F101As were produced, followed by 47 improved "C" models. The F-101A had only a limited front-line service life and all "A" and "C" models were converted to unarmed RF-101G and H reconnaissance aircraft for the Air National Guard. Reconnaissance versions of the F-101 Voodoo enjoyed a far longer service life than any other, and are perhaps the most important variants.

Night photography

Two main types were produced, the RF-101A and R-101C. Both had a lengthened and modified nose housing cameras for night photography. Totals of 35 RF-101As and 166 RF-101Cs were built, and were used extensively during the Cuban Missile Crisis and in the Vietnam War. The first RF-101A unit was the 363rd Tactical Reconnaissance Wing at Shaw AFB in South Carolina.

Wearing a typically flamboyant color scheme, this F-101 served with the 81st Tactical Fighter Wing at Bentwaters and Woodbridge, Suffolk.

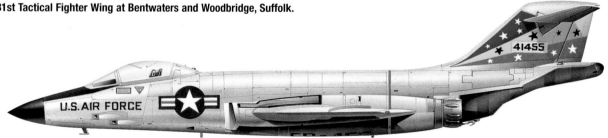

Vought F-8 Crusader

The first carrierborne fighter capable of supersonic speed in level flight, the Crusader was the winner of a 1953 US Navy competition for a new day-fighter. The prototype XF8U-1 flew on March 25, 1955, exceeding Mach One.

COUNTRY OF ORIGIN: USA

TYPE: (F-8D CRUSADER) single-seat carrier-based fighter

POWERPLANT: one 18,000lb (8165 kg) Pratt & Whitney J57-P-20 turbojet

PERFORMANCE: maximum speed at 40,000 ft (12,192 m) 1227 mph (1975 km/h); service ceiling about 59,000 ft (17,983 m); combat radius at high altitude 600 miles (966 km)

WEIGHTS: empty 19,925 lb (9038 kg); maximum take-off 34,000 lb (15,422 g)

DIMENSIONS: span 35 ft 2 in (10.72 m); length 54 ft 6 in (16.61 m); height 15 ft 9 in (4.8 m)

ARMAMENT: four .787 in (20 mm) Colt Mk 12 cannons with 144 rpg, up to four Motorola AIM-9C Sidewinder air-to-air missiles; or two AGM-12A or AGM-12B Bullpup air-to-surface missiles

The F-8 Crusader boosted the US Navy's fleet defense capability, being able to reach supersonic speed in level flight.

In 1955, Vought began the development of a totally new Crusader. Designated XF8U-3 Crusader III, the three prototypes of this aircraft were powered with various J75 engines developing up to 28,800 lb (13,064 kg) of thrust. The aircraft were able to fly at 1580 mph (2543 km/h) at a height of up to 70,000 ft (21,335 m), but to the eternal regret of many US Navy aviators, the aircraft was rejected in favor of the Phantom II. Vought continued to take the F-8 through various stages of development, hardly altering the airframe at each stage, but steadily improved the

aircraft so that it remained competitive. The most potent of all these versions was the F-8D, with J57-P-20 turbojet, extra fuel in place of the underfuselage Zuni rocket pack and new radar for a specially produced radar-homing AIM-9C Sidewinder air-to-air missile.

Clinching a deal with France

A total of 152 F-8Ds were produced. Despite failing to win export contracts for the F-8 Crusader from the Royal Navy, or for a two-seat version for the US Navy, Vought clinched a deal with the French Aéronavale for a version of the F-8E, even though her carriers *Foch* and *Clemenceau* were thought too small for such aircraft. Vought redesigned the wing and tail to provide greater lift and to improve low-speed handling. The first FN flew on June 26, 1964. All 42 were delivered by the following January.

This is an F-8U-2NE Crusader of VF-33 "Starfighters," which flew from USS *Enterprise*, the world's first nuclear-powered aircraft carrier.

Saab J-35 Draken

The Saab J-35 Draken exceeded all precedents. Designed to intercept transonic bombers at all altitudes and in all weathers, at its debut, it was a component of the finest fully integrated air-defense system in Western Europe.

Despite its potential, the Saab Draken had only limited export success. This is one of 24 examples supplied to Finland.

COUNTRY OF ORIGIN: Sweden

TYPE: single-seat all-weather interceptor

POWERPLANT: one 17,110 lb (7761 kg) Svenska Flygmotor RM6C turbojet

PERFORMANCE: maximum speed 1320 mph (2125 km/h); service ceiling 65,000 ft (20,000 m); range with maximum fuel 2020 miles (3250 km)

WEIGHTS: empty 16,369 lb (7425 kg); maximum take-off 35,274 lb (16,000 kg)

DIMENSIONS: span 30 ft 10 in (9.4 m); length 50 ft 4 in (15.4 m); height 12 ft 9 in (3.9 m); wing area 526.6 sq ft (49.20 sq m)

ARMAMENT: one 1.18 in (30 mm) Aden M/55 cannon with 90 rds, two radar-homing Rb27 and two IR-homing Rb28 Falcon air-to-air missiles, or two of four Rb24 Sidewinder AAMs, or up to 8,999 lb (4082 kg) of bombs on attack mission

The Draken was designed to a Swedish air force specification for a single-seat interceptor that could operate from short air strips, and have rapid time-to-height and supersonic performance. The aircraft, designed by Saab, led by Erik Bratt, between 1949-51 is one of the most remarkable to arrive on the post-war aviation scene.

A long aircraft
The unique "double-delta" is an ingenious method of arranging items one behind the other to give a long aircraft with small frontal area and correspondingly high aerodynamic efficiency. The aircraft was ten years in

This colorful J-35F served with the F10 Skanska Flygflottilj, being eventually replaced by the Saab Viggen.

development, with the first J35A production models arriving in service in March 1960. The major production version of the Draken was the J-35F, which was virtually designed around the Hughes HM-55 Falcon radar-guided air-to-air missile and was fitted with an improved S7B collision-course fire-control system, a high-capacity data-link system integrating the aircraft with the STRIL 60 air-defense environment, an infrared sensor under the nose and PS-01A search-and-ranging radar. The J-35C was a two-seat operational trainer, while the last new-build variant, the J-35J, was a development of the J-35D with more capable radar, collision-course fire control and a Hughes infrared sensor to allow carriage of the Hughes Falcon AAM.

Supermarine Scimitar

The Supermarine Scimitar was the end product of an evolutionary process dating back to 1945 and the Supermarine 505, a carrier-based fighter project that was revised several times.

COUNTRY OF ORIGIN: United Kingdom

TYPE: single-seat carrier-based multi-role aircraft

POWERPLANT: two 11,250 lb (5105 kg) Rolls-Royce Avon 202 turbojets

PERFORMANCE: maximum speed 710 mph (1143 km/h); service ceiling 50,000 ft (15,240 m); range, clean at height 600 miles (966 km)

WEIGHTS: empty 21,000 lb (9525 kg); maximum take-off 34,200 lb (15,513 kg)

DIMENSIONS: span 37 ft 2 in (11.33 m); length 55 ft 4 in (16.87 m); height 15 ft 3 in (4.65 m); wing area 485 sq ft (45.06 sq m)

ARMAMENT: four 1.18 in (30 mm) Aden cannons, four 1000 lb (454 kg) bombs or four Bullpup air-to-ground missiles, or four sidewinder air-to-air missiles, or drop tanks

Thanks to the position of the cockpit well forward on the nose, Scimitar pilots enjoyed excellent visibility.

The Scimitar had an extremely protracted gestation period, explained in part by the muddled procurement program, which in 1945 asked for naval fighters without normal landing gear to land on a flexible deck.

Extensive armament
The first prototype, the Supermarine 508, was a thin straight-winged design with a butterfly tail. This was changed to a conventional swept layout with cruciform tail on the 525, and finalized in the 544 with blown flaps,

The Scimitar was a far-from-ideal strike aircraft, but it provided the Royal Navy with a combined strike and interception capability.

slab tail, and area-ruled body. Three prototype Type 544 aircraft were constructed, the first of which flew in January 1956. The type was ordered into production for the Fleet Air Arm as the Scimitar F.1 and the first production aircraft flew on January 11, 1957, powered by two Rolls-Royce Avon 202 turbojets. The Scimitar became operational with No. 803 Squadron in June 1958 and three other squadrons later received the type. In 1962 the Scimitar was modified to carry the Bullpup ASM, and had provision for four Sidewinder AAMs in addition to its four 1.18 in (30 mm) cannon. The Scimitar was replaced in FAA service by the Blackburn Buccaneer and was withdrawn from first-line units by the end of 1966.

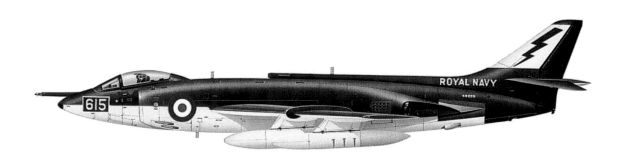

Mikoyan-Gurevich MiG-21 "Fishbed"

Known by the NATO reporting name Fishbed, the MiG-21 was a child of the Korean War: Soviet air-combat experien⬤ had demonstrated a need for a light, single-seat target defense interceptor with high supersonic maneuverability.

COUNTRY OF ORIGIN: USSR

TYPE: single-seat all-weather multi-role fighter

POWERPLANT: one 16,535 lb (7507 kg) Tumanskii R-25 turbojets

PERFORMANCE: maximum speed above 36,090 ft (11,000 m) 1385 mph (2229 km/h); service ceiling 57,400 ft (17,500 m); range on internal fuel 721 miles (1160 km)

WEIGHTS: empty 11,464 lb (5200 kg); maximum take-off 22,925 lb (10,400 kg)

DIMENSIONS: span 23 ft 5.5 in (7.15 m); length (including probe) 51 ft 8.5 in (15.76 m); height 13 ft 5.5 in (4.10 m); wing area 247.58 sq ft (23 sq m)

ARMAMENT: one .91 in (23 mm) GSh-23 twin-barrel cannon in underbelly pack, four underwing pylons with provision for about 3307 lb (1500 kg) of stores, including AA-2 Atoll or AA-8 Aphid air-to-air missiles, UV-16-57 rocket pods, napalm tanks, or drop tanks

This is a MiG-21 of No. 1 "Tiger" Squadron, Indian Air Force. It was later replaced by the Mirage 2000.

The initial production versions (Fishbed-A and –B) were built in limited numbers, being short-range day-fighters with a light armament of two 1.18 in (30 mm) NR-30 cannon. The next variant, the MiG-21F Fishbed-C, carried two K-13 Atoll infrared homing AAMs, and had an uprated Tumansky R-11 turbojet as well as improved avionics.

Widely used around the globe

The MiG-21F was the first major production version; it entered service in 1960 and was progressively modified and updated over the years that followed. In the early 1970s the MiG-21 was virtually redesigned, re-emerging as the MiG-21B (Fishbed-L) multi-role air superiority fighter and ground-attack version. The Fishbed-N of 1971 introduced new advanced construction techniques, greater fuel capacity and updated avionics for multi-role air combat and ground attack. The MiG-21 became the most widely used jet fighter in the world, being license-built in India, Czechoslovakia and China, and equipping some 25 Soviet-aligned air forces. A two-seat version, the MiG-21U, was given the NATO reporting name Mongol.

The MiG-21 was used by all the Warsaw Pact air forces. This is an example from the Hungarian Air Force.

Dassault Mirage III

One of the biggest success stories in the field of post-1945 combat aircraft design, the Dassault Mirage III owed its origin to the Dassault MD550 Mirage I of 1954.

The hugely successful Mirage program has brought incalculable prestige to the French aviation industry. The early prototype aircraft was conceived to meet an Armée de l'Air light interceptor specification of 1952. Once again Dassault found the powerplant insufficient and produced a larger, heavier and more powerful aircraft, the Mirage III.

Mach 2 in level flight

On October 24, 1958, pre-production Mirage IIIA-01 became the first West European fighter to attain Mach 2 in level flight. The production version was designated the IIIC, a slightly developed version with either guns or a booster rocket for faster climb. The Mirage IIIC was identical to the IIIA, with an Atar 09 B3 turbojet and a

A Mirage IIICZ of the South African Air Force at low level over the Veldt. South Africa was an early customer.

COUNTRY OF ORIGIN: France

TYPE: single-seat day visual fighter-bomber

POWERPLANT: one 13,668 lb (6200 kg) SNECMA Atar 9C turbojet

PERFORMANCE: maximum speed at sea level 883 mph (1390 km/h); service ceiling 55,755 ft (17,000 m); combat radius at low level with 2000 lb (907 kg) load 745 miles (1200 km)

WEIGHTS: empty 15,540 lb (7050 kg); loaded 27,760 lb (13,500 kg)

DIMENSIONS: span 26 ft 11.875 in (8.22 m); length 56 ft (16.5 m); height 14 ft 9 in (4.5 m); wing area 376.7 sq ft (35 sq m)

ARMAMENT: two .787 in (20 mm) DEFA 552A cannon with 125 rpg; three external pylons with provision for up to 6612 lb (3000 kg) of stores, including bombs, rockets and gun pods

SEPR 841 or 844 auxiliary rocket motor. The Armée de l'Air ordered 100, equipping the 2e and 13e Escadres de Chasse and 72 similar aircraft were supplied to the Israeli Air Force, the first deliveries being made to No. 101 Sqn in 1963. These aircraft were designated Mirage IIICJ and saw considerable action during the subsequent Arab-Israeli wars. The Mirage IIIE was a long-range tactical strike variant, 453 examples being produced for the Armée de l'Air and further aircraft for export.

In Israeli Air Force service, the Mirage III played a vital part in the Six-Day War of 1967, attacking enemy airfields and providing air defense.

Convair F-106 Delta Dart

To improve visibility, the F-106 had optically flat windscreen panels that met at their forward engines and had a "vision splitter," a blade-like metal structure that stopped internal reflections without obstructing the pilot's view.

COUNTRY OF ORIGIN: USA

TYPE: (F-106 DELTA DART) light-attack and reconnaissance aircraft

POWERPLANT: two 2850 lb (1293 kg) General Electric J85-GE-17A turbojets

PERFORMANCE: maximum speed at 16,000 ft (4875 m) 507 mph (816 km/h); service ceiling 41,765 ft (12,730 m); range with 4100 lb (1860 kg load) 460 miles (740 km)

WEIGHTS: empty 6211 lb (2817 kg); maximum take-off 14,000 lb (6350 kg)

DIMENSIONS: span including tip tanks 35 ft 10.25 in (10.93 m); length 28 ft 4 in (8.62 m); height 8 ft 1.33 in (2.7 m); wing area 183.9 sq ft (17.09 sq m)

ARMAMENT: one .3 in (7.62 mm) GAU-2 Minigun six-barrelled machine gun, eight underwing hardpoints with provision for more than 5000 lb (2268 kg) of stores, including bombs, rocket and gun pods, napalm tanks, and other equipment

It had a less-than-ideal weapons system, but the F-106 remained in service with the US Air Defense Command for nearly three decades.

In the early 1960s the F-106A was the most important type on the inventory of Air Defense Command, with which it served exclusively.

In 1948 Convair flew the world's first delta-wing aircraft, the XF-92A, which was part of a program meant to lead to a supersonic fighter. This was ended, but the US Air Force later issued a specification for an extremely advanced all-weather interceptor to carry the Hughes MX-1179 electronic control system. Early flight trials of the F-102 prototype were disappointing, but once the design was right, 875 were delivered.

Electronic weapons-control system

In the search mode the pilot flew with two control columns; the left hand being used to adjust the sweep angle and range of the radar. The F-106 was originally designated F-102B to indicate the strong family connection with the earlier Delta Dagger. The aircraft was designed from the outset as an integral weapon system, in which each of the differing units would integrate as a compatible system. Central to this project was an electronic weapons-control system. It had been hoped to realize this objective with the Delta Dagger, but delays in the program meant that the ECS was not ready until late in 1955, an unacceptable timescale to the USAF who planned to bring the F-102 into service that year. The F-106 was delayed by engine problems, and disappointing flight tests. The Hughes-designed MA-1 ECS was also not performing well. But the aircraft entered service in 1959 and remained in service, in updated versions, until 1988.

BAC (English Electric) Lightning

Only the RAF made the jump from subsonic to Mach Two fighter with no Mach One plus intermediary, replacing the Hawker Hunter day-fighter and the Gloster Javelin with the Mach 2 English Electric (later BAC) Lightning.

COUNTRY OF ORIGIN: United Kingdom

TYPE: (FMK 1A) single-seat all-weather interceptor

POWERPLANT: two 14,430 lb (6545 kg) Rolls-Royce Avon turbojets

PERFORMANCE: maximum speed at 36,000 ft (10.970 m) 1,500 mph (2,414 km/h); service ceiling 60,000 ft (18,920 m); range 895 miles (1440 km)

WEIGHTS: empty 28,000 lb (12,700 kg); maximum take-off 50,000 lb (22,680 kg)

DIMENSIONS: span 34 ft 10 in (10.6 m); length 53 ft 3 in (16.25 m); height 19 ft 7 in (5.95 m); wing area 380.1 sq ft (35.31 sq m)

ARMAMENT: interchangeable packs of two all-altitude Red Top or stern chase Firestreak air-to-air missiles or two 1.18 in (30 mm) Aden guns, in forward part of belly tank

The Lightning F.Mk.6 was fitted with a long under-fuselage tank to extend its range. Its lack of endurance was an ongoing problem.

Twenty pre-production aircraft were built before the first F.Mk 1 entered service in 1960. The F.Mk 1A had provision for flight refuelling and UHF radio.

Poor duration

A complicated aircraft for its day, its maintenance time per flying hour was high. The aircraft was as good as any all-weather interceptor then available, with a phenomenal top speed and rate of climb, but it was hampered by poor duration. The RAF decided to modify the much-improved F.3 to F.6 standard in 1965. The F.6 featured an extensively modified ventral tank and a cambered, kinked wing leading edge, to allow operations at greater weights.

W.E.W. "Teddy" Petter was the driving force behind the aircraft that was, during the 1960s, the world's most formidable interceptor. The Lightning developed from a prototype built by English Electric, called the P.1, which first flew in August 1954. The P.1 was powered by two Bristol Siddeley Sapphire engines mounted "under and over," and fed by a common inlet. P.1B was a completely redesigned version to meet the British government Specification F.23/49, with a two-shock intake. With Avon engines fitted, Mach 2 was attained in November 1958.

No. 56 Squadron formed the RAF Fighter Command aerobatic team, The Firebirds – named after the squadron's crest – in 1963.

Dassault Super Etendard

During the 1982 Falklands War, the Exocet-armed Super Etendard was the biggest threat to the British naval task force. It sank two ships and would doubtless have sunk more, but the missiles were in short supply.

COUNTRY OF ORIGIN: France

TYPE: single-seat carrierborne strike/attack and interceptor aircraft

POWERPLANT: one 11,023 lb (5000 kg) SNECMA Atar 8K-50 turbojet

PERFORMANCE: maximum speed 733 mph (1180 km/h) at low level; service ceiling 44,950 ft (13,700 m); combat radius 528 miles (850 km) on hi-lo-hi mission with one Exocet and two external tanks

WEIGHTS: empty 14,330 lb (6500 kg); maximum take-off 26,455 lb (12,000 kg)

DIMENSIONS: span 31 ft 6 in (9.60 m); length 46 ft 11.2 in (14.31 m); height 12 ft 8 in (3.86 m); wing area 305.7 sq ft (28.4 sq m)

ARMAMENT: two 1.18 in (30 mm) DEFA 553 cannon with 125 rpg, five external hardpoints with provision for up to 4630 lb (2100 kg) of stores, including nuclear weapons, Exocet and (Argentina only) Martin Pescador air-to-surface missiles, Magic air-to-air missiles, bombs and rockets, refuelling and reconnaissance pods

The Dassault Etendard gave the French Navy a powerful attack capability. It evolved into the Super Etendard.

Originally designed for a mid-1950s tactical strike fighter contest (which it lost to the Fiat G.91) the Dassault Etendard (Standard) showed such outstanding qualities that a development contract was awarded on behalf of the French Navy, which was looking for a strike aircraft capable also of high-altitude interception.

Resolving unexplained crashes

The navalized prototype Etendard IVM-01 flew on May 21, 1958, powered by a SNECMA Atar 8B turbojet, and began service trials the following October. The first of

69 production Etendard IVMs was delivered to the Aeronavale on January 18, 1962, being followed into service by the Etendard IVP, an unarmed reconnaissance-tanker variant. During the late 1960s it had been expected that the original Etendard force would be replaced in about 1971 by a specially developed carrier version of the Jaguar. This was rejected by the Aeronavale for political and financial reasons, and Dassault's proposal for an improved Etendard was chosen. The new aircraft had a redesigned structure, a more efficient engine, inertial navigation system and other upgraded avionics. The first prototype flew on October 3, 1975; deliveries to the Aeronavale began in June 1978. Fourteen Super Etendards were supplied to Argentina in 1981; the five delivered by the following spring were used to great effect against British shipping during the Falklands War. Five were also loaned to Iraq. The aircraft in French service are due for replacement by Rafale by 2010.

This Super Etendard wears the attractive light-and-dark-gray color scheme adopted by the French Navy.

McDonnell Douglas F-4 Phantom II

One of the most potent and versatile combat aircraft ever built, the McDonnell (later McDonnell Douglas) F-4 Phantom II stemmed from a 1954 project for an advanced naval fighter designated F3H-G/H.

F-4 Phantoms of the USAF in formation.

COUNTRY OF ORIGIN: USA

TYPE: (F-4C) two seat all-weather fighter/attack aircraft

POWERPLANT: two 17,000 lb (7718 kg) General Electric J79-GE-15 turbojets

PERFORMANCE: maximum speed at high altitude 1500 mph (2414 km/h); service ceiling 60,000 ft (18,300 m); range on internal fuel with no weapon load 1750 miles (2817 km)

WEIGHTS: empty 28,000 lb (12,700 kg); maximum take-off 58,000 lb (26,308 kg)

DIMENSIONS: span 38 ft 5 in (11.7 m); length 58 ft 3 in (17.76 m); height 16 ft 3 in (4.96 m); wing area 530 sq ft (49.24 sq m)

ARMAMENT: four AIM-7 Sparrows recessed under fuselage; two wing pylons for two AIM-7s, or four AIM-9 Sidewinders, provision for .787 in (20 mm) M-61 cannons in external centerline pod; four wing pylons for tanks, bombs, or other stores to a maximum weight of 13,500 lb (6219 kg)

The XF4H-1 Phantom prototype flew for the first time on May 27, 1958. The first fully operational Phantom squadron, VF-114, commissioned with F-4Bs in October 1961, and in June 1962 the first USMC deliveries were made to VMF(AW)-314. Total F-4B production was 649 aircraft. Twenty-nine F-4Bs were loaned to the USAF for

evaluation in 1962 and proved superior to any Air Force fighter-bomber. A production order was quickly placed for a USAF variant; this was originally designated F-110A, but later changed to F-4C. Deliveries to the USAF began in 1963, 583 aircraft being built. The RF-4B and RF-4C were unarmed reconnaissance variants for the USMC and USAF, while the F-4D was basically an F-4C with improved systems and redesigned radome.

Various versions fulfill many roles

The major production version was the F-4E, 913 of which were delivered to the USAF between 1967 and 1976. F-4E export orders totalled 558. The RF-4E was the tactical reconnaissance version. The F-4F (175 built) was a version for the Luftwaffe, intended for the air superiority role, while the F-4G Wild Weasel was the F4E modified for the suppression of enemy defense systems. The successor to the F-4B in USN/USMC service was the F-4J, which possessed greater ground-attack capability; the first of 522 production aircraft was delivered in June 1976. The first foreign nation to order the Phantom was Great Britain, the British aircraft being powered by Rolls-Royce RB168-25R Spey 201 engines. The Japanese Air Self-Defense Force equipped five squadrons with 140 Phantom F-4EJs, and the RAAF leased 24 F-4Es in 1970. Phantoms were delivered to Spain, Greece and Turkey, so that by the mid-1970s several key NATO air forces were standardized on the type.

This F-4 Phantom, operated by the US Navy's Fighter Squadron VF-84, was called the "Jolly Rogers," hence the skull and crossbones.

Avro Canada CF-105 Arrow

The CF-105 delta-wing all-weather interceptor flew for the first time on March 25, 1958. Four more aircraft were built and four more were almost completed when the project was abruptly cancelled in 1959.

COUNTRY OF ORIGIN: Canada

TYPE: two-seat all-weather long-range supersonic interceptor

POWERPLANT: two 23,500 lb (10,659 kg) Pratt & Whitney J75-P-3 turbojets

PERFORMANCE: Mach 2.3 recorded during tests

WEIGHTS: empty 49,040 lb (22,244 kg); average take-off during trials 57,000 lb (25,855 kg)

DIMENSIONS: span 50 ft (15.24 m); length 77 ft 9.75 in (23.72 m); height 21 ft 3 in (6.48 m); wing area 113.8 sq m (1,225 sq ft)

ARMAMENT: eight Sparrow air-to-air missiles in internal bay

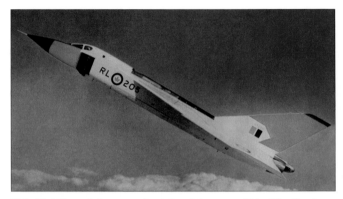

This CF-105 carried some red paintwork for ease of identification in the event of an emergency during Arctic trials.

The story of the Arrow bears a startling similarity to that of the BAC TSR.2. Both projects showed great promise during the early stages of development in the mid-1950s, and both were destroyed by the misguided decisions of politicians who were convinced that the days of the manned interceptor were numbered.

Significant contribution to aviation technology

The first stages of development of the Arrow, a two-seat all-weather interceptor, began in 1953, with planned entry into service as a replacement for the same company's CF-100. Production of the first five prototypes began in April 1954. The design had a huge high-set delta wing. The first flight of the aircraft was made on March 25, 1958, but just under 10 months later the project was cancelled. All the prototypes were destroyed in what must rank as one of the most short-sighted decisions made by any Canadian government. The CF-105 was one of the most advanced interceptors in the world, but escalating development costs and an offer by the US government to equip three RCAF air defense squadrons with the F-101B Voodoo brought about its demise. But during its brief career, it had made a significant contribution to aviation technology.

The powerful and heavily armed CF-105 Arrow had an excellent design, but fell victim to escalating development costs.

Northrop F-5A Freedom Fighter

It was announced on April 25, 1962, that the Northrop N156, first flown in 1959, had been selected as the new all-purpose fighter for friendly nations under the Mutual Aid Pact, and the aircraft entered production as the F-5A.

COUNTRY OF ORIGIN: USA

TYPE: light tactical fighter

POWERPLANT: two 4080 lb (1850 kg) General Electric J85-GE-13 turbojets

PERFORMANCE: maximum speed at 36,000 ft (10,975 m) 924 mph (1487 km/h); service ceiling 50,500 ft (15,390 m); combat radius with maximum warload 195 miles (314 km)

WEIGHTS: empty 8085 lb (3667 kg); maximum take-off 20,667 lb (9374 kg)

DIMENSIONS: span 25 ft 3 in (7.7 m); length 47 ft 2 in (14.38 m); height 13 ft 2 in (4.01 m); wing area 170 sq ft (15.79 sq m)

ARMAMENT: two .787 in (20 mm) M39 cannon with 280 rpg; provision for 4400 lb (1996 kg) of stores on external pylons, (including two air-to-air missiles on wingtip pylons), bombs, cluster bombs and rocket launcher pods

During its career the F-5 Freedom Fighter was used by 36 air forces around the world. This example is Turkish.

In 1955, Northrop began the design of a lightweight fighter powered by two underslung J85 missile engines. This was yet another of the countless projects born during the Korean era when pilots were calling for lighter, simpler fighters with higher performance.

Supplied on advantageous terms

The team led by Welko Gasich refined the design, putting the engines in the fuselage and increasing their size. The F-5A, largely a privately funded project by Northrop, was developed from the T-38 Talon. In October 1962 the US

The USAF used the F-5 in the "aggressor" role, its small size approximating that of Russia's MiG-21.

Department of Defense decided to buy the aircraft in large numbers to supply to friendly countries on advantageous terms. More than 1000 were supplied to Iran, Taiwan, Greece, South Korea, Philippines, Turkey, Ethiopia, Morocco, Norway, Thailand, Libya and South Vietnam. The first overseas customer was the Imperial Iranian Air Force, followed by the Royal Hellenic and Royal Norwegian Air Forces. Between 1965 and 1970 Canadair built 115 aircraft for the Canadian Armed Forces as CF-5A/Ds, these using Orenda-built J85-CAN-15 engines. An improved version, the F-5E Tiger II, was selected in November 1970 as a successor to the F-5A series. It served with a dozen overseas air forces, and also in the "aggressor" air-combat training role with the USAF. The RF-5E TigerEye was a photo-reconnaissance version.

BAe/McDonnell Douglas AV-8B Harrier II

The Harrier II traces its lineage back to 1957, when Hawker Siddeley Aircraft Ltd. launched the concept of the P.1127 V/STOL aircraft, designed around the Bristol BE.53 vectored-thrust engine.

COUNTRY OF ORIGIN: USA and UK

TYPE: V/STOL close-support aircraft

POWERPLANT: one 23,800 lb (10,796 kg) Rolls Royce F402-RR-408 Pegasus vectored thrust turbofan

PERFORMANCE: maximum speed at sea level 661 mph (1065 km/h); service ceiling more than 50,000 ft (15,240 m); combat radius with 6000 lb (2722 kg) bomb load 172 miles (277 km)

WEIGHTS: empty 13,086 lb (5936 kg); maximum take-off 31,000 lb (14,061 kg)

DIMENSIONS: span 30 ft 4 in (9.25 m); length 46 ft 4 in (14.12 m); height 11 ft 7.75 in (3.55 m); wing area 230 sq ft (21.37 sq m)

ARMAMENT: one .98 in (25 mm) GAU-12U cannon; six external hardpoints with provision for up to 17,000 lb (7711 kg) (Short take-off) or 7000 lb (3175 kg) (Vertical take-off) of stores, including AAMs, ASMs, freefall or guided bombs, cluster bombs, dispenser weapons, napalm tanks, rocket launchers and ECM pods

The Harrier II is a far more powerful and effective aircraft than the original Harrier, with massive combat potential in the close-support role.

A development of the P.1127, the Kestrel was evaluated in 1965 by pilots of the RAF, US Air Force, US Navy, US Army, and the Federal German Luftwaffe. The aircraft was selected by the RAF and, named Harrier GR.1, entered service on April 1, 1969. This, the world's first operational V/STOL aircraft, was followed by the GR.1A and GR.3, the latter having a nose-mounted laser rangefinder and uprated Pegasus Mk 103 engine.

Flown by the US Marine Corps

In 1966 six Kestrels were sent to the USA for tri-service trials on land and sea under the designation XV-6A, and in 1969 the US Marine Corps bought the first of 102 aircraft, with the designation AV-8A. The AV-8B version of the Harrier was developed for the US Marine Corps, who had a requirement for a single-seat close support aircraft to supersede the AV-8A Harriers. The was a collaboration between the two companies, who had each sought to improve on the Harrier design. The first of four full-scale development aircraft was flown on November 5, 1981. The design team made used carbon fiber in many of the major structural components, introduced a range of lift augmenting devices, redesigned the control surface, redesigned the cockpit/forward fuselage, and added two additional wing hardpoints. The aircraft entered service with the Marine Corps in January 1985. The RAF's GR7 Harriers are essentially AV-8Bs with RAF electronics and weapons fit. The Spanish navy operate a version of the AV-8A, designated AV-8G Matador.

Seen here is a Harrier GR.3 of No. 3 Squadron RAF, which operated the type in Germany from 1972.

Mikoyan-Gurevich MiG-25 Foxbat

During the 1991 Gulf War, a MiG-25 was the only Iraqi aircraft to score an aerial victory, shooting down an F/A-18 Hornet. MiG-25s proved capable of outrunning both the F-15 Eagle and the latter's AIM-7 air-to-air missiles.

The MiG-25 was developed to counter the threat from projected American supersonic bombers armed with stand-off missiles.

COUNTRY OF ORIGIN: USSR

TYPE: single-seat interceptor

POWERPLANT: two 22,487 lb (10,200 kg) Tumanskii R-15B-300 turbojets

PERFORMANCE: maximum speed at altitude about 1848 mph (2974 km/h); service ceiling over 80,000 ft (24,385 m); combat radius 702 miles (1130 km)

WEIGHTS: empty 44,092 lb (20,000 kg); maximum take-off 82,508 lb (37,425kg)

DIMENSIONS: span 45 ft 11.75 in (14.02 m); length 78 ft 1.75 in (23.82 m); height 20 ft 0.5 in (6.10 m); wing area 660.9 sq ft (61.40 sq m)

ARMAMENT: external pylons for four air-to-air missiles in the form of either two each of the IR- and radar-homing AA-6 "Acrid," or two AA-7 "Apex" and two AA-8 "Aphid" weapons

Reports of the development of a long-range, high-speed strategic bomber in the US in the late 1950s (the B-70 Valkyrie) prompted the Soviet authorities to design and develop an interceptor that could be operational to meet the B-70s planned 1964 in-service date. Even when the B-70 program was cancelled in 1961, work continued on the development of the interceptor known as the MiG-25, given the NATO reporting name "Foxbat."

Setting world records

The aircraft was unveiled publicly at the 1967 Moscow Aviation Day. The prototypes blazed a trail of world records in 1965–67, and when the MiG-25P production aircraft entered service in 1970 it far outclassed any Western aircraft in speed and height. The MiG-25R, MiG-25RB and MiG-25BM are derivatives of the MiG-25P. The MiG-25R, as its suffix implies, is a reconnaissance variant, while the MiG-25RB has a high-level bombing capability. The MiG-25BM variant can launch guided missiles against ground targets. The MiG-25 interceptor is gradually being replaced in first-line service by a greatly improved version, the MiG-31. First flown on September 16, 1975, as the Ye-155MP, and originally designated MiG-25MP, the MiG-31 (known by the NATO reporting name "Foxhound") entered production in 1975 and the first units to arm with the type became operational in 1982, replacing MiG-23s and Su-15s.

Its day as an interceptor over, the MiG-25 found a new role as a high-speed, high-altitude reconnaissance aircraft.

Vought A-7 Corsair II

Development of the A-7 Corsair II was extremely rapid, losses sustained by the A-4 Skyhawk squadrons in Vietnam making it imperative to introduce the new type into combat as quickly as possible.

COUNTRY OF ORIGIN: USA

TYPE: single-seat attack aircraft

POWERPLANT: one 14,250 lb (6465 kg) Allison TF41-1 (Rolls-Royce Spey) turbofan

PERFORMANCE: maximum speed at low-level 698 mph (1123 km/h); combat range with typical weapon load 4100 miles (1150 km)

WEIGHTS: empty 19,781 lb (8972 kg); maximum take-off 42,000 lb (19,050 kg)

DIMENSIONS: span 38 ft 9 in (11.8 m); length 46 ft 1.5 in (14.06 m); height 16 ft 0.75 in (4.9 m); wing area 375 sq ft (34.84 sq m)

ARMAMENT: one .787 in (20 mm) M61 Vulcan with 1000 rounds, external pylons with provision for up to 15,000 lb (6804 kg) of stores, including guided and conventional bombs, cluster bombs, napalm tanks, air-to-surface missiles and drop tanks

Many A-7D Corsair IIs, like this example, were assigned to Air National Guard units.

Though derived from the Vought F-8 Crusader, the Corsair is a totally different aircraft. By restricting performance to high subsonic speed it was possible to reduce structural weight dramatically, and correspondingly the range increased dramatically and weapon load multiplied by nearly four. The prototype flew for the first time on September 27, 1965. The first attack variant was the A-7A, which made its combat debut in the Gulf of Tonkin on December 4, 1966, with Attack Squadron VA-147, operating from the USS *Ranger*. Also deployed to South-East Asia was the A-7E, a close support/interdiction variant developed for the US Navy. By the end of the conflict in Vietnam, A-7s had flown more than 100,000 combat missions. In all, 199 A-7As were delivered before production switched to the A-7B, which had an uprated engine. The first production model flew on February 6,

1968, the USN taking delivery of 198 examples. The next variant was the A-7D tactical fighter for the USAF, which went into action in Vietnam in October 1972; 459 were built, many being allocated to Air National Guard units.

Low attrition rate

The latter began taking delivery of the A-7D in October 1975, when the 188th Tactical Fighter Squadron at Kirtland AFB received its first aircraft. In total, 14 ANG squadrons operated the type and achieved an enviably low attrition rate. The final major Corsair variant, the two-seat A-7K, served only with the ANG. Corsair IIs were also operated by the Hellenic, Portuguese and Thai air forces.

This A-7D formed part of the *John F. Kennedy* carrier air group. The A-7 made its combat debut in Vietnam.

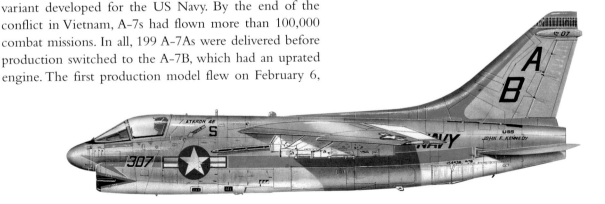

Mikoyan-Gurevich MiG-23/27 Flogger

The MiG-23, which flew in prototype form in 1967 and entered service with the Frontal Aviation's attack units of the 16th Air Army in Germany in 1973, was the Soviet Air Force's first true multi-role combat aircraft.

COUNTRY OF ORIGIN: USSR

TYPE: (Flogger-E) single-seat air combat fighter

POWERPLANT: one 22,046 lb (10,000 kg) Tumanskii R–27F2M-300 turbojet

PERFORMANCE: maximum speed at altitude about 1520 mph (2445 km/h); service ceiling over 60,000 ft (18,290 m); combat radius on hi-lo-hi mission 600 miles (966 km)

WEIGHTS: empty 22,932 lb (10,400 kg); maximum loaded 40,000 lb (18,145 kg)

DIMENSIONS: wingspan 45 ft 10 in (13.97 m) spread and 25 ft 6.25 in (7.78 m) swept; length (including probe) 54 ft 10 in (16.71 m); height 15 ft 9.75 in (4.82 m); wing area 402 sq ft (37.25 sq m) spread

ARMAMENT: one .91 in (23 mm) GSh-23L cannon with 200 rounds, six external hardpoints with provision for up to 6614 lb (3000 kg) of stores, including AA-2 Atoll air-to-air missiles, cannon pods, rocket-launcher pods, large caliber rockets and bombs

The Indian Air Force was one overseas customer for the MiG-23/27 Flogger, the first example being delivered in 1980.

The MiG-23 was a variable-geometry fighter-bomber with wings sweeping from 23 to 71 degrees, and was the Soviet Air Force's first true multi-role combat aircraft. The MiG-23M Flogger-B was the first series production version and equipped all the major Warsaw Pact air forces; a simplified version for export to Libya and other Middle East air forces was designated MiG-23MS Flogger-E. The MiG-23UB Flogger-C was a two-seat trainer, retaining the combat capability of the single-seat variants, while the MiG-23BN/BM Flogger-F and -H were fighter-bomber versions for export.

Battlefield support variant

The MiG-27, which began to enter service in the late 1970s, was a dedicated battlefield support variant known to NATO as Flogger-D; the MiG-27D and -27K Flogger-J were improved versions, while the MiG-23P was a dedicated air defense variant. About 5000 MiG-23/27s were built, and in the 1990s the type was in service with 20 air forces.

Pictured is a Flogger of the Egyptian Air Force. Some were acquired by the USAF for evaluation.

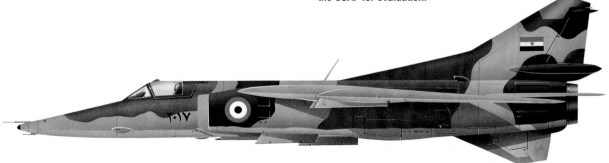

Saab Viggen (Thunderbolt)

Until the Panavia Tornado, the Saab Viggen was the most advanced combat aircraft ever produced in Europe, with a far more advanced radar, greater speed range and a more comprehensive avionics fit than its contemporaries.

The Viggen was a true multi-role combat aircraft, being able to undertake air-to-air, air-to-ground and reconnaissance roles.

COUNTRY OF ORIGIN: Sweden

TYPE: (AJ37) single-seat all-weather attack aircraft

POWERPLANT: one 26,015 lb (11,800 kg) Volvo Flygmotor RM8 turbofan

PERFORMANCE: maximum speed at high altitude 1320 mph (2124 km/h); service ceiling 60,000 ft (18,290 m); combat radius on hi-lo-hi mission with external armament 621 miles (1000 km)

WEIGHTS: empty 26,015 lb (11,800 kg); maximum take-off 45,194 lb (20,500 kg)

DIMENSIONS: span 34 ft 9.25 in (10.6 m); length 53 ft 5.75 in (16.3 m); height 18 ft 4.5 in (5.6 m); wing area 495.16 sq ft (46 sq m)

ARMAMENT: seven external hardpoints with provision for 13,228 lb (6000 kg) of stores, including 1.18 in (30 mm) Aden cannon pods, 5.315 in (135 mm) rocket pods, Sidewinder or Falcon air-to-air missiles for self-defense, Maverick air-to-surface missiles, bombs, and cluster bombs

The Saab 37 Viggen (Thunderbolt) was designed to carry out the four roles of attack, interception, reconnaissance and training. Like the earlier J35 Draken, it was fully integrated into the STRIL 60 air-defense control system. Powered by a Swedish version of the Pratt & Whitney JT8D turbofan engine, with a powerful Swedish-developed afterburner, the aircraft had excellent acceleration and climb performance.

Using motorways as runways
Part of the requirement was that it should be capable of operating from sections of Swedish motorways. The first of seven prototypes flew on February 8, 1967, followed by the first production AJ37 single-seat all-weather attack variant in February 1971. Deliveries of the first of 110

AJ37s to the Royal Swedish Air Force began in June that year. The AJ37 interceptor version of the Viggen (149 built), replaced the J35F Draken; the SF37 (26 delivered) was a single-seat armed photo reconnaissance variant; and the SH37 (26 delivered) was an all-weather maritime reconnaissance version, replacing the S32C Lansen. The SK37 (18 delivered) was a tandem two-seat trainer, retaining a secondary attack role.

This JA37 Viggen carries the number 21 on its nose, denoting that it belonged to Flygflottilj 21 at Lulea.

Grumman F-14 Tomcat

The variable-geometry F-14 Tomcat, one of the most formidable interceptors of all time, was designed to gain complete air superiority in the vicinity of a carrier task force and attack tactical objectives as a secondary role.

COUNTRY OF ORIGIN: USA

TYPE: (F-14D) two-seat carrierborne fleet defense fighter

POWERPLANT: two 27,000 lb (12,247 kg) General Electric F110-GE-400 turbofans

PERFORMANCE: maximum speed at high altitude 1241 mph (1988 km/h); service ceiling 53,000 ft (16,150 m); range about 1239 miles (1994 km) with full weapon load

WEIGHTS: empty 41,780 lb (18,951 kg); maximum take-off 74,349 lb (33,724 kg)

DIMENSIONS: wingspan 64 ft 1.5 in (19.55 m) unswept; 38 ft 2.5 in (11.65 m) swept; length 62 ft 8 in (19.1 m); height 16 ft (4.88 m); wing area 565 sq ft (52.49 sq m)

ARMAMENT: one .787 in (20 mm) M61A1 Vulcan rotary cannon with 675 rounds; external pylons for a combination of AIM-7 Sparrow medium range air-to-air missiles, AIM-9 medium range air-to-air missiles, and AIM-54A/B/C Phoenix long range air-to-air missiles

The variable-geometry F-14 provided an effective round-the-clock air defense system for the US Navy's carrier task groups.

Selected in January 1969 as the winner of a US Navy contest for a carrierborne fighter (VFX), the prototype F14A flew for the first time on December 21, 1970, and was followed by 11 development aircraft. The variable-geometry fighter completed carrier trials in 1972 and deliveries to the US Navy began in October that year, the Tomcat forming the interceptor element of a carrier air wing. Development of the production F-14A was hampered by the loss of the prototype in December 1970, but 478 aircraft were supplied to the US Navy in total, and 80 more F-14As were exported to Iran in the later 1970s. The F-14B, a proposed version with Pratt & Whitney F401P400 turbofans, was cancelled, but 32 F-14As were fitted with the General Electric F110-GE-400 and redesignated F-14B. The F-14D was an improved version with more powerful radar, enhanced avionics, a redesigned cockpit and a tactical jamming system; 37 aircraft were built from new and 18 converted from F-14As.

Clashes with Libyan fighters

In the 1980s the Tomcat was involved in several clashes with Libyan fighters over the Gulf of Sirte. During the Gulf War of 1991 the type shared the air combat patrol task with the McDonnell Douglas F-15 Eagle. Since then the type has seen active service in the Balkans and Afghanistan, and again in Iraq in 2003. The Tomcat was retired from US Navy service in September 2006.

This F-14 Tomcat of Fighter Squadron VF-143 has an insignia depicting a winged griffon with its head lowered, which earned the squadron its nickname of the "Pukin' Dogs."

Yakovlev Yak-38 Forger

The Yak-38 Forger came as a surprise to NATO when it first appeared aboard the aircraft carrier Kiev, passing through the Mediterranean in the summer of 1976. It was never in the same league as Britain's Harrier.

COUNTRY OF ORIGIN: USSR

TYPE: V/STOL carrier-based fighter-bomber

POWERPLANT: two 6724 lb (3050 kg) Rybinsk RD-36-35VFR lift turbojets; one 15,322 lb (6950 kg) Tumanskii R-27V-300 vectored-thrust turbojet

PERFORMANCE: maximum speed at high altitude 627 mph (1009 km/h); service ceiling 39,370 ft (12,000 m); combat range on hi-lo-hi mission with maximum weapon load 230 miles (370 km)

WEIGHTS: empty 16,502 lb (7485 kg); maximum take-off 25,795 lb (11,700 kg)

DIMENSIONS: span 24 ft (7.32 m); length 50 ft 10 in (15.5 m); height 14 ft 4 in (4.37 m); wing area 199.14 sq ft (18.5 sq m)

ARMAMENT: four external hardpoints with provision for 4409 lb (2000 kg) of stores, including air-to-air missiles, air-to-surface missiles, bombs, rocket-launcher pods, cannon pods and drop tanks

A Yak-38 hovering over the deck of a Russian aircraft carrier. The aircraft had a high accident rate.

The first prototype of the USSR's first (and so far only) STOVL carrierborne fighter-bomber, named Forger by NATO, flew in 1971 and the Yak-38 (originally designated the Yak-36M) first appeared to the West in July 1976 when the aircraft carrier Kiev deployed with a development squadron of Forger-As and passed through the Mediterranean en route to join the Northern Fleet.

Fleet defense, reconnaissance, anti-ship striker

The normal complement for the Kiev-class through deck aircraft carrier was a dozen single-seat Forger-As and one or two twin-seat trainer Yak-38U Forger-Bs. The primary roles were fleet defense, reconnaissance and anti-ship strike. The Forger was retired from front-line service in 1992-93, but a few remained in the inventory for another year. A total of 231 aircraft had been built by the time production ended in 1988. The Yak-38U was a trainer version. Unlike the British Harrier, which used a single vectored-thrust turbojet engine, the Yak-38 used two fixed turbojets mounted in the forward fuselage to provide vertical lift, a third engine with vectored thrust nozzles providing forward thrust. The wing folded for carrier stowage, and was fitted with wingip reaction controls.

Although it performed adequately, the Yak-38 was never an outstanding aircraft.

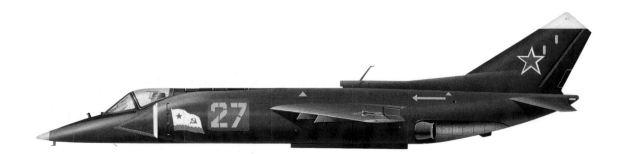

McDonnell Douglas F-15

The F-15 Eagle was designed to outperform, outfly and outfight any opponent it might encounter in the foreseeable future, in engagements extending from beyond visual range (BVR) down to close-in turning combat.

COUNTRY OF ORIGIN: USA

TYPE: single-seat air superiority fighter with secondary strike/attack role

POWERPLANT: two 23,810 lb (10,885 kg) Pratt & Whitney F100-PW-100 turbofans

PERFORMANCE: maximum speed at high altitude 1650 mph (2655 km/h); initial climb rate over 50,000 ft (15,240 m)/min; ceiling 100,000 ft (30,500 m); range on internal fuel 1200 miles (1930 km)

WEIGHTS: empty 28,000 lb (12,700 kg); with maximum load 56,000 lb (25,424 kg)

DIMENSIONS: span 42 ft 9.75 in (13.05 m); length 63 ft 9 in (19.43 m); height 18 ft 5 in (5.63 m); wing area 608 sq ft (56.48 sq m)

ARMAMENT: one .787 in (20 mm) M61A1 cannon with 960 rounds, external pylons with provision for up to 16,800 lb (7620 kg) of stores, for example four AIM-7 Sparrow air-to-air missiles and four AIM-9 Sidewinder AAMs; when configured for attack role conventional and guided bombs, rockets, air-to-surface missiles; tanks and/or ECM pods

This is an F-15E Strike Eagle shown flying over a bombing range in the USA. The F-15E has phenomenal striking power.

McDonnell Douglas produced the F-15 Eagle to succeed the F-4 Phantom in US service. Since its inception, this aircraft has assumed the crown as the world's greatest air superiority fighter, but it has now been superseded by later F-15C and F-15B variants in US service. The first prototype of the F-15A, a single-seat twin-turbofan swept-wing aircraft flew in July 1972. The powerful Pratt & Whitney engines and extensive use of titanium in construction enabled sustained high speeds (Mach 2.5 plus) at high altitude. Deliveries began to the 555th Tactical Fighter Training Wing at Langley AFB, Virginia, in November 1974.

This F-15E Strike Eagle serves with the 48th Tactical Fighter Wing at Lakenheath, Suffolk.

Supplied to Israel and Saudi Arabia

Production continued until 1979 with 385 built. The tandem-seat F-15B was developed alongside the F-15A, and the main production version was the F-15C. The latter was built under license in Japan as the F-15J. The F-15 was supplied to Israel as the F-15I and to Saudi Arabia as the F-15S. The F-15E Strike Eagle is a dedicated strike/attack variant, and has seen much action in Iraq, Afghanistan and elsewhere.

General Dynamics (Lockheed Martin) F-16

The F-16 Fighting Falcon, now produced by Lockheed Martin, is the world's most prolific combat aircraft, with over 2000 in service with the United States Air Force and a further 2000 in service with 19 other air forces.

COUNTRY OF ORIGIN: USA

TYPE: single-seat air superiority fighter with secondary strike/attack role

POWERPLANT: two 23,810 lb (10,885 kg) Pratt & Whitney F100-PW-100 turbofans

PERFORMANCE: maximum speed at high altitude 1650 mph (2655 km/h); initial climb rate over 50,000 ft (15,240 m)/min; ceiling 100,000 ft (30,500 m); range on internal fuel 1200 miles (1930 km)

WEIGHTS: empty 28,000 lb (12,700 kg); with maximum load 56,000 lb (25,424 kg)

DIMENSIONS: span 42 ft 9.75 in (13.05 m); length 63 ft 9 in (19.43 m); height 18 ft 5 in (5.63 m); wing area 608 sq ft (56.48 sq m)

ARMAMENT: one .787 in (20 mm) M61A1 cannon with 960 rounds, external pylons with provision for up to 16,800 lb (7620 kg) of stores, for example, four AIM-7 Sparrow air-to-air missiles and four AIM-9 Sidewinder AAMs; when configured for attack role conventional and guided bombs, rockets, air-to-surface missiles; tanks and/or ECM pods

The F-16 brought a high degree of versatility when it entered service with the air forces of NATO and other friendly nations.

The F-16, designed and built by General Dynamics first flew on February 2, 1974. The F-16B and F-16D are two-seat versions, while the F-16C, delivered from 1988, had many improvements in avionics and was available with a choice of engine. F-16s have seen action in the Lebanon (with the Israeli Air Force), in the Gulf wars and the Balkans. A typical stores load might include two wingtip-mounted Sidewinders, with four more on the outer underwing stations; a podded GPU-5/A 30mm cannon on the centerline; drop tanks on the inboard underwing and fuselage stations; a Pave Penny laser spot tracker pod along the starboard side of the nacelle; and bombs, ASMs and flare pods on the four inner underwing stations.

Beyond-visual-range missiles

The aircraft can carry advanced beyond-visual-range missiles, Maverick ASMs, HARM and Shrike anti-radar missiles, and a weapons dispenser carrying various types of sub-munition including runway denial bombs, shaped-charge bomblets, anti-tank and area denial mines.

Among the 24 overseas air forces using the F-16 is that of Pakistan, one of whose aircraft is pictured here.

Mikoyan-Gurevitch MiG-29 Fulcrum

The MiG-29 Fulcrum and another Russian fighter, the Sukhoi Su-27 Flanker, were designed in response to the F-15 and its naval counterpart, the Grumman F-14 Tomcat.

COUNTRY OF ORIGIN: USSR

TYPE: single-seat air-superiority fighter with secondary ground attack capability

POWERPLANT: two 18,298 lb (8300 kg) Sarkisov RD-33 turbofans

PERFORMANCE: maximum speed ceiling 55,775 ft (17,000 m); range with internal fuel 932 miles (1500 km)

WEIGHTS: empty 24,030 lb (10,900 kg); maximum take-off 40,785 lb (18,500 kg)

DIMENSIONS: wingspan 37 ft 3.75 in (11.36 m); length (including probe) 56 ft 10 in (17.32 m); height 25 ft 6.25 in (7.78 m); wing area 378.9 sq ft (35.2 sq m)

ARMAMENT: one 1.18 in (30 mm) GSh-30 cannon with 150 rounds, eight external hardpoints with provision for up to 9921 lb (4500 kg) of stores, including six AA-11 "Archer" and AA-10 "Alamo" infra-red or radar guided air-to-air missiles, rocket-launcher pods, large caliber rockets, napalm tanks, drop tanks, ECM pods, conventional and guided bombs

The MiG-29 Fulcrum, seen here in Polish Air Force insignia, came as a big surprise to NATO when it first appeared.

Both Russian aircraft share a similar configuration, combining a wing swept at 40 degrees with highly swept wing root extensions, underslung engines with wedge intakes, and twin fins. The Fulcrum-A became operational in 1985. The MiG-29K is a navalized version, the MiG-29M is a variant with advanced fly-by-wire systems, and the MiG-29UB is a two-seat operational trainer. The MiG-29 is the first aircraft in the world to be fitted with dual-mode air intakes. During flight, the open air intakes feed air to the engines in the normal way, but while the aircraft is taxiing the air intakes are closed and air is fed through the louvres on the upper surface of the wing root to prevent ingestion of foreign objects from the runway – important when operating from unprepared airstrips.

Detecting faraway targets

The aircraft has an RP-29 pulse-Doppler radar capable of detecting targets at around 100km (62 miles) away. Fire control and mission computers link the radar with a laser rangefinder and infra-red search/track sensor, in conjunction with a helmet-mounted target designator. The radar can track ten targets simultaneously, and the system allows the MiG-29 to approach and engage targets without emitting detectable radar or radio signals. The Russian Air Force has begun to upgrade 150 of its MiG-29 fighters, which will be designated MiG-29SMT. A two-seater version, the MiG-29M2, has also been shown, as has a super-maneuverable MiG-29OVT, with three-dimensional thrust-vectoring engine nozzles.

This MiG-29 was used for carrier trials. Note the lowered arrester hook. The navalized variant was known as the MiG-29K.

Sukhoi Su-27 Flanker

The Sukhoi Su-27, like the F-15, is a dual-role aircraft; in addition to its primary air superiority task it was designed to escort Su-24 Fencer strike aircraft on deep penetration missions.

COUNTRY OF ORIGIN: USSR

TYPE: two-seat strike and attack aircraft

POWERPLANT: two 24,802 lb (11,250 kg) Lyul'ka AL-21F-3A turbojets

PERFORMANCE: maximum speed above 36,090 ft (11,000 m) approximately 1,439 mph (2316 km/h); service ceiling 57,415 ft (17,500 m); combat radius on hi-lo-hi mission with 6614 lb (3000 kg) load 650 miles (1050 km)

WEIGHTS: empty 41,888 lb (19,000 kg); maximum take-off 87,520 lb (39,700 kg)

DIMENSIONS: wingspan 57 ft 10 in (17.63 m) spread and 34 ft (10.36 m) swept; length 80 ft 5 in (24.53 m); height 16 ft 0.75 in (4.97 m); wing area 452.1 sq ft (42 sq m)

ARMAMENT: one .91 in (23 mm) GSh-23-6 six-barrelled cannon; nine external pylons with provision for up to 17,635 lb (8000 kg) of stores, including nuclear weapons, air-to-air missiles, air-to-surface missiles such as the AS-14 "Kedge," guided bombs, cluster bombs, dispenser weapons, large-caliber rockets, rocket-launcher pods, drop tanks and ECM pods

This Su-27 is seen undergoing deck compatibility trials aboard the aircraft carrier *Admiral Kuznetsov*.

The Su-27 prototype flew for the first time in May 1977, the type being allocated the code name Flanker by NATO. Full-scale production of the Su-27P Flanker-B air defense fighter began in 1980, and the aircraft became operational in 1984. Like its contemporary, the MiG-29 Fulcrum, the Su-27 combines a wing swept at 40 degrees with highly swept wing root extensions, underslung engines with wedge intakes, and twin fins. The combination of modest wing sweep with highly swept root extensions, is designed to enhance maneuverability and generate lift, making it possible to achieve extraordinary angles of attack. The Su-27UB Flanker-C is a two-seat training version. The Sukhoi Su-35, derived from the Flanker-B and originally designated Su-27M, is a second-generation version with improved agility and enhanced operational capability.

This Su-27C Flanker-B of the 24th Guards Fighter Regiment, Kubinka, wears the striking pre-1997 color scheme of the Russki Vityazi (Russian Knights) aerobatic team.

Dassault Mirage 2000C

Development of the Mirage 2000 was started after the failure of a collaborative program, the Anglo-French Variable Geometry Aircraft, and of a number of subsequent projects involving VG aircraft of purely French design.

COUNTRY OF ORIGIN: France

TYPE: single-seat air-superiority and attack fighter

POWERPLANT: one 21,834 lb (9700 kg) SNECMA M53-P2 turbofan

PERFORMANCE: maximum speed at high altitude 1,453 mph (2338 km/h); service ceiling 59,055 ft (18,000 m); range with 2,205 lb (1000 kg) load 920 miles (1,480 km)

WEIGHTS: empty 16,534 lb (7500 kg); maximum take-off 37,480 lb (17,000 kg)

DIMENSIONS: span 29 ft 11.5 in (9.13 m); length 47 ft 1.25 in (14.36 m); height 17 ft 0.75 in (5.20 m); wing area 441.3 sq ft (41 sq m)

ARMAMENT: two DEFA 554 cannons with 125 rpg; nine external pylons with provision for up to 13,890 lb (6300 kg) of stores, including R.530 air-to-air missiles, AS.30 or A.30L missiles, rocket-launcher pods, and various attack loads including 1000 lb (450 kg) bombs. For air-defense weapon training the Cubic Corpn AIS (airborne instrumentation subsystem) pod, which resembles a Magic missile, may be carried

This Indian Air Force Mirage 2000 carries the crest of No. 7 Squadron "The Battleaxes" on its nose.

Early research and experience had shown that the delta wing configuration had disadvantages, not least a lack of low speed maneuverability. With the development of fly-by-wire technology during the late 1960s and early 1970s, it was possible for airframe designers to overcome some of these problems, when coupled with advances in aerodynamics. The 2000C was designed by Dassault to be a single-seat interceptor to replace the F.1. The aircraft was adopted by the French government in December 1975 as the primary combat aircraft of the French air force. It was developed initially under contract as an interceptor and air-superiority fighter. Deliveries to the Armée de l'Air began in July 1984; early examples were fitted with the SNEMCA M53-5; aircraft built later have the more powerful M53-P2.

Mirage IIIE replacement

The Mirage 2000N, first flown in February 1983, was developed as a replacement for the Mirage IIIE and is armed with the ASMP medium-range nuclear missile. This version (75 delivered from 1987) is strengthened for operations at 690 mph (1110 km/h) at 200 ft (60 m). Like its predecessors, the Mirage 2000 has been the subject of substantial export orders from Abu Dhabi, Egypt, Greece, India and Peru. In Indian Air Force service the aircraft, designated Mirage 2000H, is known as the Vajra (Thunderstreak).

Ten Mirage 2000P fighters, one pictured here, were delivered to Peru, along with two Mirage 2000DP trainers.

McDonnell Douglas F/A-18 Hornet

While the F-14 replaced the Phantom in the naval air-superiority role, the aircraft that replaced it in the tactical role (with both the USN and USMC) was the McDonnell Douglas F-18 Hornet.

COUNTRY OF ORIGIN: USA

TYPE: (F/A-18A) single-seat fighter and strike aircraft

POWERPLANT: two 16,000 lb (7264 kg) General Electric F404-GE-400 turbofans

PERFORMANCE: maximum speed at 40,000 ft (12,190 m) 1183 mph (1912 km/h); combat ceiling 50,000 ft (15,240 m); combat radius 662 miles (1065 km)

WEIGHTS: empty 23,050 lb (10,455 kg); maximum take-off 56,000 lb (25,401 kg)

DIMENSIONS: span 37 ft 6 in (11.43 m); length 56 ft (17.07 m); height 15 ft 3.5 in (4.66 m); wing area 400 sq ft (37.16 sq m)

ARMAMENT: one .787 in (20 mm) M61A1 Vulcan rotary cannon with 570 rounds; nine external hardpoints with provision for up to 17,000 kg (7711 kg) of stores, including air-to-air missiles, air-to-surface missiles, anti-ship missiles, free-fall or guided bombs, cluster bombs, dispenser weapons, napalm tanks, rocket launchers, drop tanks and ECM pods

Afterburners blazing, an F/A-18 Hornet is catapulted from the deck of a US aircraft carrier.

In the early 1970s the US Navy had a requirement for a lightweight, inexpensive carrier-based aircraft that could be adapted for a variety of roles and used in conjunction with the more sophisticated and heavier Grumman F-14 Tomcat and as a replacement for the F-4 Phantom II and Vought A-7 Corsair II aircraft. The Hornet was originally derived from the private venture Northrop YF-17. Northrop undertook development work in conjunction with McDonnell Douglas and are also involved in production. Although the aircraft was originally to have been produced in both fighter and attack versions, service aircraft are easily adapted to either role. Deliveries began in May 1980 to the US Navy and were completed in 1987.

Aging fighters

On April 10, 1980, the Canadian Armed Forces minister announced his country's decision to buy 138 single-seat F-18A and 40 tandem-seat F-18B aircraft, to replace its aging CF-104 Starfighters. The order for the single-seat F-18A was progressively cut back to 98, but deliveries of trainer aircraft, designated CF-18B, began in October 1982. Each squadron operates a mixture of the two types, to enhance its multi-role capability. An enlarged new version, the F/A-18E/F Super Hornet, replacing the F/A-18C/Ds is now in service.

This is an F/A-18 Hornet of US Navy Fighter-Attack Squadron VFA-87, the "Golden Warriors," which converted to the Hornet from the A-7 in 1986.

Panavia Tornado ADV

The first Tornado ADV squadron, No. 29, formed at RAF Coningsby in 1987 and was declared operational in November. The aircraft armed seven squadrons in addition to No. 229 OCU (which became No. 56 Reserve Squadron).

With afterburners blazing, the Tornado ADV prototype takes off from the British Aerospace airfield at Warton, Lancashire, UK.

COUNTRY OF ORIGIN: Germany, Italy and UK

TYPE: all-weather air-defense aircraft

POWERPLANT: two 16,520 lb (7493 kg) Turbo-Union RB.199-34R Mk 104 turbofans

PERFORMANCE: maximum speed above 36,090 ft (11,000 m) 1452 mph (2337 km/h); operational ceiling about 70,000 ft (21,335 m); intercept radius more than 1150 miles (1853 km)

WEIGHTS: empty 31,970 lb (14,501 kg); maximum take-off 61,700 lb (27,987 kg)

DIMENSIONS: span 45 ft 7.75 in (13.91 m) spread and 28 ft 2.5 in (8.6 m); swept length 61 ft 3 in (18.68 m); height 19 ft 6.25 in (5.95 m); wing area 286.3 sq ft (26.60 sq m)

ARMAMENT: two 1.06 in (27 mm) IWKA-Mauser cannon with 180 rpg, six external hardpoints with provision for up to 12,800 lb (5806 kg) of stores, including Sky Flash medium-range air-to-air missiles, AIM-9L Sidewinder short range air-to-air missiles and drop tanks

In the late 1960s the RAF saw the need to replace its McDonnell Douglas Phantom II and BAe Lighting interceptors, and ordered the development of the Tornado ADV (Air Defense Variant), a dedicated air-defense aircraft with all-weather capability. To attain adequate fighter performance the designers had to recess the BAe Sky Flash air-to-air missile under the fuselage centerline. Full development was authorized in March 1976, and the aircraft shares 80 percent commonality with its predecessor. Structural changes include a lengthened nose for the Foxhunter radar, and a slight increase in the fuselage length. Deliveries of 18 F2s to the RAF were followed by 155 F3 aircraft with Mk 104 engines. The aircraft was sold to Saudi Arabia and Italy has leased 24 ex-RAF F3s for air cover until the Eurofighter enters service. Normal air-defense operations with the Tornado

F3 involve a "heavy combat fit," which means four Sky Flash, four Sidewinders and no external tanks.

Successful intervention

A good example of what the F3 can achieve without the long-range tanks was given on September 10, 1988, when two aircraft of No. 5 Squadron were scrambled from RAF Coningsby to intercept a pair of Tupolev Tu-95 Bear-D maritime radar reconnaissance aircraft over the Norwegian Sea. A VC-10 tanker was scrambled from RAF Leuchars to rendezvous with the Tornados, which carried out the intercept successfully.

The Royal Saudi Air Force, one of whose aircraft is pictured here, was the major export customer for the ADV.

Dassault Rafale

Developed at huge cost, the Dassault Rafale is the result of France's "go it alone" policy, and is designed for both land- and carrier-based service.

COUNTRY OF ORIGIN: France

TYPE: carrier-based multi-role combat aircraft

POWERPLANT: two 16,424 lb (7450 kg) SNECMA M88-2 turbofans

PERFORMANCE: maximum speed at high altitude 1324 mph (2130 km/h); combat radius air-to-air mission 1152 miles (1853 km)

WEIGHTS: empty equipped 21,600 lb (9800 kg); maximum take-off 42,990 lb (19,500 kg)

DIMENSIONS: span 35 ft 9.175 in (10.90 m); length 50 ft 2.5 in (15.30 m); height 17 ft 6.25 in (5.34 m); wing area 495.1 sq ft (46 sq m)

ARMAMENT: one 1.18 in (30 mm) DEFA 791B cannon, 14 external hardpoints with provision for up to 13,228 lb (6000 kg) of stores, including air-to-air missiles, air-to-surface missiles, anti-ship missiles, guided and conventional bombs, rocket launchers, recce, Elint and jammer pods

Rafale can carry a substantial load of weapons and fuel tanks, as shown in this photograph.

France, a member of the European consortium set up to develop Eurofighter, decided early on to withdraw and develop her own agile combat aircraft for the twenty-first century. The result was the Dassault Rafale (Squall).

Wide-ranging destroyer

Known first as the ACX (Avion de Combat Experimental), the main characteristics of the prototype were shown in 1983, when it was announced that the type would replace the SEPECAT Jaguar in French Air Force service some time in the 1990s. As the ACM (Avion de Combat Marine) it would form a major component of the air groups to be deployed on the French Navy's new generation of nuclear-powered aircraft carriers. On the basis of an airframe with overall dimensions little greater than those of the Mirage 2000, Dassault set out to produce a multi-role aircraft capable of destroying anything from supersonic aircraft to helicopters in the air-to-air role, and able to deliver at least 7715 lb (3500 kg) of bombs of modern weapons on targets up to 400 miles (650 km) from its base. The three versions are the Rafale A single-seater, the Rafale B two-seat multi-role aircraft and the Rafale M naval fighter variant.

The first Rafale M navalized fighter variant, seen here, was delivered to the French Navy in 2001.

Saab JAS 39 Gripen

Despite some teething troubles, Saab's JAS-39 Gripen is proving to be an excellent multi-role combat aircraft, and is competing with Eurofighter and Rafale in the lucrative export market.

COUNTRY OF ORIGIN: Sweden

TYPE: single-seat all-weather fighter, attack and reconnaissance aircraft

POWERPLANT: one 18,100 lb (8210 kg) Volvo Flygmotor RM12 turbofan

PERFORMANCE: maximum speed more than Mach 2; range on hi-lo-hi mission with external armament 2020 miles (3250 km)

WEIGHTS: empty 14,600 lb (6622 kg); maximum take-off 27,500 lb (12,473 kg)

DIMENSIONS: span 26 ft 3 in (8 m); length 46 ft 3 in (14.1 m); height 15 ft 5 in (4.7 m)

ARMAMENT: one 1.06 in (27 mm) Mauser BK27 cannon with 90 rounds, six external hardpoints with provision for Rb71 Sky Flash and Rb24 Sidewinder air-to-air missiles, Maverick air-to-surface missiles, Rb15F anti-ship missiles, bombs, cluster bombs, rocket-launcher pods, reconnaissance pods, drop tanks and ECM pods

A Gripen is shown here cruising high above the mountainous terrain of northern Sweden.

Saab has produced another excellent lightweight fighter in the form of the Gripen. The aircraft was conceived during the late 1970s as a replacement for the AJ, SH, SF and JA versions of the Saab 37 Viggen. Configuration follows Saab's tried-and-tested convention with an aft-mounted delta and swept canard foreplanes. The flying surfaces are controlled via a fly-by-wire system. Advanced avionics, including pulse-Doppler search and acquisition radar, pod-mounted FLIR, head-up and -down displays

This is a JAS 39A Gripen of Flygflottilj 7, Skaraborgs, Sweden.

(replacing normal flight instruments) and excellent ECM and navigation systems, give the aircraft multi-role all-weather capability.

Hardened against birdstrike

The aircraft's Volvo Flygmotor RM.12 turbofan (a license-built General Electric GE F404) is hardened against birdstrike. Despite the fact that Sweden's impact on the military aircraft export market to date has not been spectacular, the Gripen has registered one major success; on December 3, 1999, the South African Air Force announced that Saab and British Aerospace would supply 28 Gripens and 24 Hawk 100s, to be delivered between 2005 and 2012. The Gripen is also in service with the Czech Republic Air Force and the Hungarian Air Force.

Lockheed Martin F-22 Raptor

This was the most exciting combat aircraft of the early twenty-first century. In the 1970s, the USAF required 750 examples of a tactical aircraft that would stay viable for the first quarter of the new century.

COUNTRY OF ORIGIN: USA

TYPE: single-seat supersonic air-superiority fighter

POWERPLANT: two 35,000 lb (15,876 kg) Pratt & Whitney F119-P-100 turbofans

PERFORMANCE: maximum speed 1451 mph (2335 km/h); service ceiling 65,000 ft (19,812 m); combat radius 800 miles (1285 km)

WEIGHTS: empty 31,000 lb (14,061 kg); maximum take-off 60,000 lb (27,216 kg)

DIMENSIONS: span 43 ft (13.1 m); length 64 ft 2 in (19.55 m); height 17 ft 8 in (5.39 m); wing area 830 sq ft (77.1 sq m)

ARMAMENT: production aircraft will have cannon armament plus next generation air-to-air missiles in the internal weapons bay

The F-22 Raptor is a powerful addition to America's air superiority arsenal, but it was acquired at horrendous cost.

In April 1991, after a tightly fought competition to find a replacement for the F-15 Eagle, the Pratt & Whitney powered F-22 proposed by the Lockheed/Boeing partnership was declared the winner. The aircraft incorporates all of the most advanced avionics and airframe technology, such as stealth, a long-range supersonic combat radius, high agility and STOL capability, and an advanced nav/attack system using artificial intelligence to filter data and so reduce the pilot's workload. The definitive airframe design was achieved in March 1992. Following an assessment of the aircraft's combat role in 1993, it was decided to add a ground-attack capability. To this end, the internal weapons bay can also accommodate 454 kg (1,000 lb) GBU-32 precision guided missiles. The F-22 is designed for a high sortie rate, with a turnround time of under twenty minutes, and its avionics are highly integrated to provide rapid reaction in air combat, much of its survivability depending on the pilot's ability to locate a target very early and kill it with a first shot.

Engaging aircraft

The F-22 was designed to meet a specific threat, which at that time was presented by large numbers of highly agile Soviet combat aircraft, its task being to engage them in their own airspace with beyond visual-range weaponry. As the F-22A, the aircraft became operational with the 1st Fighter Wing at Langley AFB, Virginia, in December 2005.

This is the first YF-22 prototype, which flew in 1990.

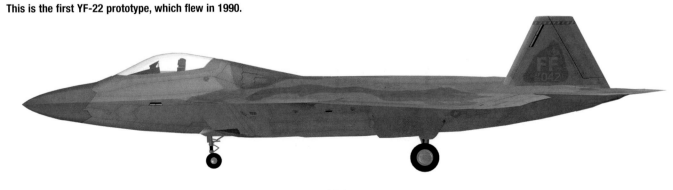

Eurofighter Typhoon

Eurofighter is a "pilot's airplane," with emphasis on the best possible all-around visibility and comfort in high-g maneuvers. The pilot's head-mounted sight avoids the need to pull tight turns to achieve missile lock-on.

COUNTRY OF ORIGIN: Germany, Italy, Spain and United Kingdom

TYPE: multi-role fighter

POWERPLANT: two 20,250 lb (9185 kg) Eurojet EJ200 turbofans

PERFORMANCE: maximum speed at 36,090 ft (11,000 m) 1,321 mph (2125 km/h); combat radius 288 and 345 miles (463 and 556 km)

WEIGHTS: empty 21,495 lb (9750 kg); maximum take-off 46,297 lb (21,000 kg)

DIMENSIONS: span 34 ft 5.5 in (10.50 m); length 47 ft 4 in (14.50 m); height 13 ft 1.5 in (4.0 m); wing area 564.05 sq ft (52.4 sq m)

ARMAMENT: one 1.06 in (27 mm) Mauser cannon; thirteen fuselage hardpoints for a wide variety of stores including ASRAAM, AMRAAM missile programs; also air-to-surface missiles, anti-radar missiles, guided and unguided bombs

Seen here is a Eurofighter Typhoon F.2 of No. 29 Squadron, which forms part of the Typhoon wing at RAF Coningsby, Lincolnshire.

The agreement to develop the Eurofighter was signed in May 1988 between the UK, the former West Germany and Italy. Spain joined in November. The aircraft was designed ostensibly for the air-to-air role, with secondary air-to-surface capability.

Supremely maneuverable

With the canard design and fly-by-wire control system the aircraft is supremely maneuverable in the air. Other advanced features include extensive use of composite materials and an advanced sensor and avionics suite. The

One of the development aircraft, Typhoon ZH588 features a roundel incorporating the national colors of the participating nations.

first two Eurofighter prototypes flew in 1994. The original customer requirement was 250 each for the UK and Germany, 165 for Italy and 100 for Spain. The latter country announced a firm requirement for eighty-seven in 1994, while Germany and Italy revised their respective needs to 180 and 121. The UK's order was 232, with options on a further sixty-five. Deliveries to the air forces of all four countries were scheduled to begin in 2001, but not for the first time the schedule slipped. The RAF received its first Eurofighter Typhoon Mk 1 on June 30, 2003. Eurofighter has broken into the export market with an Austrian order for 35 aircraft.

Lockheed Martin F-35

The X-35A Joint Strike Fighter project originated in a 1980s requirement by the US Marine Corps and the Royal Navy that a replacement for the Sea Harrier and AV-8B would be needed early in the twenty-first century.

COUNTRY OF ORIGIN: USA

TYPE: joint strike fighter

POWERPLANT: One 42,000 lb (19,026 kg) thrust Pratt & Whitney F119-PW-611S turbofan and one 18,000 lb (8154 kg) thrust Rolls-Royce lift fan (X-35B only)

PERFORMANCE: Max speed Mach 1.4+ at altitude; service ceiling 50,000+ ft (15,240+ m); combat radius 621 miles (1000 km)

WEIGHTS: 50,000 lb (22,680 kg) loaded

DIMENSIONS: span 33 ft (10.05 m); length 50 ft 11 in (15.52 m); height not known

ARMAMENT: Six AIM-120C AMRAAM or two AIM-120C AMRAAM and two 2,000 lb (907 kg) JDAM in internal fuselage bay; provision for one .787 in (20 mm) M61A2 rotary cannon with 400 rounds in starboard wing root (USAF CTOL variant). Provision for 4 underwing pylons with 5000 lb (2268 kg) of stores each.

The Lockheed Martin F-35 is a very ambitious combat aircraft project, and was developed throughout the decade of the 1990s.

The F-35 originated in a program called the Common Affordable Lightweight Fighter (CALF) project, aimed at producing a single aircraft design with both STOVL and Conventional Take-Off and Landing (CTOL) variants. In March 1993, study contracts were issued to Lockheed and McDonnell Douglas under the CALF project. In addition, Boeing and Northrop Grumman initiated private venture design studies. In 1995, CALF was absorbed into the Joint Advanced Strike Technology (JAST) program, which was originally intended to focus on technology studies and demonstration of various equipment for next-generation strike aircraft.

Joint Strike Fighter

In fact, JAST soon evolved into a firm requirement for an advanced single-seat, single-engined lightweight multi-role fighter that could be operated by the USAF, US Navy and US Marines in closely similar variants. In 1996 JAST was renamed JSF (Joint Strike Fighter), and in November that year Boeing and Lockheed Martin were awarded contracts to build two Concept Demonstrator Aircraft (CDA), one CTOL version and one STOVL version, each.

For the two CDA aircraft, the designation X-35A was allocated to the CTOL version and X-35B to the STOVL version. Unlike Boeing, Lockheed Martin introduced a third version, the X-35C, to undertake simulated aircraft carrier testing. The X-35A and X-35B have very similar airframes, including the aft cockpit bulge and associated doors for the lift-fan, which is only fitted to the X-35B. The Lockheed Martin X-35A made its first flight on October 24, 2000, from Palmdale, California.

The F-35 is by no means an attractive aircraft, but it is highly functional, with state-of-the-art systems.

Glossary

AAM Air-to-Air Missile.

AEW Airborne Early Warning.

afterburning (reheat) Method of increasing the thrust of a gas turbine aircraft engine by injecting additional fuel into the hot exhaust duct between the engine and the tailpipe, where it ignites to provide a short-term increase of power.

aileron An aerofoil used for causing an aircraft to roll around its longitudinal axis, usually fitted near the wingtips.

all-up weight The total weight of an aircraft in operating condition. Normal maximum AUW is the maximum at which an aircraft is permitted to fly within normal design restrictions, while overload weight is the maximum AUW at which an aircraft is permitted to fly subject to ultimate flying restrictions.

altimeter Instrument that measures altitude, or height above sea level.

angle of attack The angle between the wing (airfoil) and the airflow relative to it.

aspect ratio The ratio of wing span to chord.

ASV Air to Surface Vessel – airborne detection radar for locating ships and submarines.

ATF Advanced Tactical Fighter.

AWACS Airborne Warning and Control System.

basic weight The tare weight of an aircraft plus the specified operational load.

center of gravity Point in a body through which the sum of the weights of all its parts passes. A body suspended from this point is said to be in a state of equilibrium.

center of pressure Point through which the lifting force of a wing acts.

charged particle beam A stream of charged atomic particles of intense energy, focused on a target.

chord Cross-section of a wing from leading edge to trailing edge.

delta wing Aircraft shaped like the Greek letter delta.

disposable load The weight of crew and consumable load (fuel, missiles etc.).

empty equipped (also known as Tare Weight) The weight of an aircraft equipped to a minimum scale, i.e. with all equipment plus the weight of coolant in the engines, radiators and associated systems, and residual fuel in tanks, engines and associated systems.

FGA Fighter Ground Attack.

FRS Fighter Reconnaissance Strike.

gas turbine Engine in which burning fuel supplies hot gas to spin a turbine.

GPS Global Positioning System. A system of navigational satellites.

GR General Reconnaissance.

interdiction Deep air strikes into enemy areas to sever communications with the battlefield.

landing weight The AUW of an aircraft at the moment of landing.

mach Named after the Austrian professor Ernst Mach, a Mach number is the ratio of the speed of an aircraft or missile to the local speed of sound. At sea level, Mach One (1.0M) is approximately 762 mph/h (1226 km), decreasing to about 660mph/h (1062 km) at 30,000 feet. An aircraft or missile travelling faster than Mach One is said to be supersonic.

maximum landing weight The maximum AUW, due to design or operational limitations, at which an aircraft is permitted to land.

maximum take-off weight The maximum AUW, due to design or operational limitations, at which an aircraft is permitted to take off.

muzzle velocity The speed at which a bullet or shell leaves a gun barrel.

NBC Nuclear, Chemical and Biological (warfare).

NVG Night Vision Goggles. Specially designed goggles that enhance a pilot's ability to see at night.

operational load The weight of equipment necessarily carried by an aircraft for a particular role.

payload The weight of passengers and/or cargo.

rudder Movable vertical surface or surfaces forming part of the tail unit, by which the yawing of an aircraft is controlled.

SAM Surface-to-Air Missile.

stall Condition that occurs when the smooth flow of the air over an aircraft's wing changes to a turbulent flow and the lift decreases to the point where control is lost.

stealth technology Technology applied to aircraft or fighting vehicles to reduce their radar signatures.

STOVL Short Take-off, Vertical Landing.

take-off weight The AUW of an aircraft at the moment of take-off.

thermal imager Equipment fitted to an aircraft or fighting vehicle that typically comprises a telescope to collect and focus infra-red energy emitted by objects on a battlefield, a mechanism to scan the scene across an array of heat-sensitive detectors, and a processor to turn the signals from these detectors into a "thermal image" displayed on a TV screen.

turbofan engine Type of jet engine fitted with a very large front fan that not only sends air into the engine for combustion but also around the engine to produce additional thrust. This results in faster and more fuel-efficient propulsion.

turbojet engine Jet engine that derives its thrust from a stream of hot exhaust gases.

turboprop engine Jet engine that derives its thrust partly from a jet of exhaust gases, but mainly from a propeller powered by a turbine in the jet exhaust.

variable-geometry wing A type of wing whose angle of sweep can be altered to suit a particular flight profile. Popularly called a Swing Wing.

VHF Very High Frequency.

VLF Very Low Frequency.

V/STOL Vertical/Short Take-off and Landing.

yaw The action of turning an aircraft in the air around its normal (vertical) axis using the rudder. An aircraft is said to yaw when the fore-and-aft axis turns to port or starboard, out of the line of flight.

For More Information

Canada Aviation Museum
P.O. Box 9724, Station T
Ottawa, ON K1G 5A3
Canada
(613) 993-2010
Web site: http://www.aviation.technomuses.ca
This museum contains both civilian and military aircraft, as well as exhibits related to Canadian aviation.

Canadian Aviation Historical Society
National Headquarters
P.O. Box 705, Station P
Toronto, ON M5S 2Y4
Canada
Web site: http://www.cahs.ca/
This organization is dedicated to preserving Canada's aviation history.

Dryden Flight Research Center
P.O. Box 273
Edwards, CA 93523-0273
(661) 276-3311
Web site: http://www.nasa.gov/centers/dryden/home/index.html
The Dryden Flight Research Center is dedicated to advancing aircraft design and the science of aeronautics.

Museum of Flight
9404 East Marginal Way South
Seattle, WA 98108-4097
(206) 764-5720
Web site: http://www.museumofflight.org
The Museum of Flight has many exhibitions and is home to a large aviation archive. It also features informational programs for the public.

National Air and Space Museum
6th and Independence Ave SW
Washington, DC 20560
(203) 633-1000
Web site: http://www.nasm.si.edu
The National Air and Space Museum is home to the world's largest collection of airplanes and spacecraft.

National Museum of the U.S. Air Force
1100 Spaatz Street
Wright-Patterson AFB, OH 45433
(937) 255-3286
Web site: http://www.nationalmuseum.af.mil
The National Museum of the U.S. Air Force is dedicated to preserving U.S. military aviation history.

National Naval Aviation Museum
1750 Radford Boulevard, Suite C
Naval Air Station
Pensacola, FL 32508
(850) 452-3604
(850) 452-3606
Web site: http://www.navalaviationmuseum.org
The National Naval Aviation Museum documents the history of U.S. naval military aviation. It has many aircraft in its collection.

Web Sites
Due to the changing nature of Internet links, Rosen Publishing has developed an online list of Web sites related to the subject of this book. This site is updated regularly. Please use this link to access the list:

http://www.rosenlinks.com/grw/figh

For Further Reading

Basmadjian, E. E. *The B-2 Spirit*. New York, NY: Rosen Publishing, 2003.

Boyne, Walter J. *World War II Aircraft: Great American Fighter Planes of the Second World War*. San Diego, CA: Thunder Bay Press, 2006.

Casil, Amy Sterling. *The B-1 Lancer*. New York, NY: Rosen Publishing, 2003.

Chant, Chris. *Allied Fighters 1939–1945*. Minneapolis, MN: Zenith Press, 2008.

Dartford, Mark. *Fighter Planes*. Minneapolis, MN: Lerner Publications Company, 2003.

Fiscus, James W., ed. *Critical Perspectives on World War II*. New York, NY: Rosen Publishing, 2005.

Gardner, Adrian. *The F-14 Tomcat*. New York, NY: Rosen Publishing, 2003.

Gordon, Yefim. *Soviet Air Power in World War 2*. Osceola, WI: 2008.

Grant, R.G. *Flight: 100 Years of Aviation*. New York, NY: DK Publishing, 2007.

Green, William, and Gordon Swanborough. *The Great Book of Fighters: An Illustrated Encyclopedia of Every Fighter Aircraft Built and Flown*. Osceola, WI: MBI Publishing Company, 2001.

Harris, Stephen L. *Harlem's Hell Fighters: The African-American 369th Infantry in World War I*. Dulles, VA: Brassy's, Inc., 2003.

Heppenheimer, T. A. *Flight: A History of Aviation in Photographs*. Buffalo, NY: Firefly Book, 2004.

Jackson, Robert. *101 Great Bombers*. New York, NY: Rosen Publishing, 2010.

Jakab, Peter L., and Tom D. Crouch. *The Wright Brothers and the Invention of the Aerial Age*. Washington D.C.: National Geographic, Smithsonian National Air and Space Museum, 2003.

Jeffrey, Gary. *The History of Flight*. New York, NY: Rosen Publishing, 2008.

Milstein, Jeffrey, Walter J. Boyne, and Ariel Shanberg. *AirCraft: The Jet as Art*. New York, NY: Harry N. Abrams, Inc., 2007.

Parsons, Dave, George Hall, and Bob Lawson. *Grumman F-14 Tomcat*. St. Paul, MN: Zenith Press, 2006.

Seidman, David. *The F/A-18 Hornet*. New York, NY: Rosen Publishing, 2003.

West, David. *Fighter Pilots*. New York, NY: Rosen Publishing, 2008.

Winchester, Jim, ed. *The Encyclopedia of Modern Aircraft: From Civilian Airliners to Military Superfighters*. San Diego, CA: Thunder Bay Press, 2006.

Winchester, Jim. *World's Worst Aircraft*. New York, NY: Rosen Publishing, 2008.

Yenne, Bill. *The American Aircraft Factory in World War II*. St. Paul, MN: Zenith Press, 2006.

Yenne, Bill. *Attack of the Drones: A History of Unmanned Aerial Combat*. St. Paul, MN: MBI Publishing Company, 2004.

Index

About the Editor

Robert Jackson is the author of over 80 books on military, aviation, naval and scientific subjects. He was a defense and science correspondent for a major British newspaper publishing group. His expertise has led to books covering major studies of all aspects of individual campaigns and wars.